THE ASCENSION

Lenten
Companion

A Personal Encounter with the Power of the Gospel

YEAR C

Fr. Mark Toups

ASCENSION

West Chester, Pennsylvania

Nihil obstat: Reverend S. Brice Higginbotham
                  Censor Librorum
                  September 27, 2021

Imprimatur: +Most Reverend Shelton J. Fabre
                  Bishop of Houma-Thibodaux
                  September 27, 2021

Ascension
PO Box 1990
West Chester, PA 19380
1-800-376-0520
ascensionpress.com

Cover art: Mike Moyers (*Fireside* © 2022 Mike Moyers, Franklin, TN)
Interior art: Mike Moyers *(Wilderness, Down the Mountain, Parable of the Fig Tree, Parable of the Prodigal, Neither Do I Condemn You, Christ & Pilate, Descent, Race to the Tomb* © 2022 Mike Moyers, Franklin, TN)

Printed in United States of America
ISBN 978-1-954881-09-9

CONTENTS

GETTING THE MOST OUT OF
THE ASCENSION LENTEN COMPANION

The journal you have in your hands is the third in a series of Lenten prayer journals by Fr. Mark Toups with artwork by Mike Moyers. Its purpose is to help you draw closer to Jesus Christ through daily reflections and guided prayers based on the Sunday Gospel readings.

The journal is meant to be used with video presentations by Fr. Toups, which are freely available at **ascensionpress.com/lentencompanion.** The videos and journals are ideal for use by parishes, small groups, and individuals during Lent.

Community

Community is a key component of the journey to holiness. Lent provides a wonderful opportunity to take more time for prayer and grow stronger in friendship with others on the shared journey to heaven.

The ideal is for a whole parish to take up the *Lenten Companion* and journey together as a community. You can find out how to provide journals to a large parish group at **ascensionpress.com/lentencompanion,** which also includes information about how to buy in bulk and run parish events with the *Lenten Companion* videos and journal.

If you are not able to experience the *Lenten Companion* as a whole parish, consider a small group setting. Use the *Lenten Companion* as a family devotion for Lent, or get together with a few friends to discuss how God is speaking to you during this season. Bulk pricing for small groups is also available.

You can also take this journey through Lent even if you are not meeting in a group or talking about it with friends. The *Lenten Companion* is well suited to use by individuals. Remember that you are not alone—Catholics all over the country are on the same journey. This journal is a place for you to speak to God and to hear and see all that he has to show you.

Videos

To accompany the journal, the *Lenten Companion* offers videos with Fr. Mark Toups. Through his witness, spiritual direction, and prayer, you will find fresh insights into the profound love the Lord pours out for us in his passion, death, and resurrection.

The eight videos are for Ash Wednesday, the five weeks of Lent, Holy Week, and the Triduum. These videos are available on DVD and can, in addition, be viewed anytime at **ascensionpress.com/lentencompanion**—where you can also sign up to get them sent to your inbox each week.

Daily Meditation and Prayer

The *Lenten Companion* is organized around the Sunday Gospel readings of Lent Cycle C. Each day, a new meditation invites you to draw closer to Jesus as you accompany him through the Gospel events.

You will notice that the meditations are grouped by week and that each start on a Thursday. This puts the Sunday Gospel reading right at the center of the week's meditations. In this way, meditations from Thursday through Saturday help you prepare your heart for the Gospel you will hear proclaimed at Mass on Sunday, and the remaining meditations, through Wednesday, further unpack the same Gospel reading.

Each meditation is followed by a spiritual exercise titled "For Your Prayer." Through the first five weeks of Lent, this section asks you to reflect on the Sunday Gospel or a related passage and invites you to encounter the Lord in his love as you pray. Some of these spiritual exercises are intentionally repeated to encourage you to venture more deeply into prayer. This time you spend in prayer with the Lord is the true heart of the *Lenten Companion*.

During Holy Week, the meditations shift to guided imaginative prayers. These are drawn from the events of Christ's passion and death and provide longer, more detailed scenes as the settings for your prayer.

Here are some helpful tips for praying with Scripture.

Prepare

When you are praying with Scripture, open your Bible and read the passage once. If you are praying imaginatively, read through the scene. Get familiar with the words. Then, slowly read the text a second time.

Pay attention to how you feel as you read. Pay attention to which words strike you. When the text sets a scene, enter the scene with Mary and Joseph or the other people mentioned. Once the passage or the scene comes to its natural conclusion, continue with ARRR.

ARRR

ARRR stands for **acknowledge, relate, receive, and respond.**

You have sat with God's Word. You have entered the scene. Now, when you feel that God is saying something to you, *acknowledge what stirs within you.* Pay attention to your thoughts, feelings, and desires. These are important.

After acknowledging what is going on in your heart, *relate that to God.* Don't just think about your thoughts, feelings, and desires. Don't just think about God or how God might react. Relate to God. Tell him how you feel. Tell him what you think. Tell him what you want. Share all your thoughts, feelings, and desires with God. Share everything with him.

Once you have shared everything with God, *receive from him.* Listen to what he is telling you. It could be a subtle voice you hear. It could be a memory that pops up. Maybe he invites you to reread the Scripture passage. Perhaps he invites you into a still, restful silence. Trust that God is listening to you, and receive what he wants to share with you.

Now *respond to him.* Your response could be continuing your conversation with God. It could be resolving to do something. It could be tears or laughter. Respond to what you are receiving.

Journal

The last step is to *journal.* Keep a record of your prayer this Lent. Your journal entry does not have to be lengthy. It could be a single word, a sentence or two about what God told you, or how the day's reflection struck you. However you do it, journaling will help you walk closer to God this Lent. We have provided journaling space for you each day.

Commit

As you dedicate yourself to prayer this Lent, there is no better safeguard than a good plan. We recommend the five Ws as a method of prayer planning. Here is how it works. Every Sunday, look at your calendar and write out your plan for the next six days, answering the following questions: When? Where? What? Who? and Why?

> WHEN will I spend time with Jesus?
>
> WHERE will I spend time with Jesus?
>
> WHAT are Jesus and I going to do together?
>
> WHO will hold me accountable for my time with Jesus?
>
> WHY am I prioritizing my time with Jesus?

Making a commitment is the first step in transforming your prayer life. These weeks with *The Ascension Lenten Companion – Year C* are the perfect time to begin.

Introduction

In 1976, the Catholic community of Philadelphia hosted the 41st International Eucharistic Congress, which brought Catholics together from around the world. Speakers included Dorothy Day, Mother Teresa, President Gerald Ford, and Fr. Pedro Arrupe, SJ.

Fr. Arrupe was the Superior General of the Society of Jesus, the Jesuits. It is said that after giving an impassioned speech about the importance of falling in love with God, an unconvinced naysayer scoffed, saying something akin to "That's great, but give me something practical." Without skipping a beat, Fr. Arrupe is said to have quoted fellow Jesuit Joseph Whelan as he said:

> Nothing is more practical than finding God, than falling in Love in a quite absolute, final way. What you are in love with, what seizes your imagination, will affect everything. It will decide what will get you out of bed in the morning, what you do with your evenings, how you spend your weekends, what you read, whom you know, what breaks your heart, and what amazes you with joy and gratitude. Fall in Love, stay in love, and it will decide everything.[1]

Fall in love. Stay in love. And it will decide everything. This, perhaps, is the key to the Gospel and the essence of our Faith in Jesus Christ. This, perhaps, is the key to Lent and the invitation to us over these next forty-plus days. I invite you to rethink why exactly you are reading this book. Perhaps there is a desire for more than you think. Perhaps this Lent there is more, for God is inviting you to fall in love and stay in love, so that it decides everything.

In his landmark encyclical *Deus Caritas Est* (God Is Love), Pope Benedict XVI wrote that the central fact of Christianity is the encounter with Jesus:

> *We have come to believe in God's love*: in these words the Christian can express the fundamental decision of his life. Being Christian is not the result of an ethical choice or a lofty idea, but the encounter with an event, a person, which gives life a new horizon and a decisive direction."[2]

Being Christian is not just about us or our choice for Jesus. It is about God and his choice for us. Being Christian is not about rules or regulations and what you can or cannot do. Being Christian, in its purest form, is about our encounter with a man, a real man, namely, Jesus Christ.

This is another way of saying that being Christian is about falling in love and staying in love, so that our love for Jesus Christ decides everything.

Imagine a world where Christians were so in love with Jesus Christ that their love for God decided everything in their lives. Imagine a Church where Catholics were so in love with Jesus Christ that their love for God decided everything in their lives. Imagine a Lent where ordinary people like you and me fell so in love with Jesus Christ that their love for God decided everything in their lives.

* * *

Before we move on, I would like to draw your attention to two intentional aspects of this book.

First, in each of the daily meditations, I offer you approximately five hundred words of reflection, with an additional twenty-five to fifty words in the "For Your Prayer" section. When I wrote this book, I felt the Lord asking for this Lent to be different. If we are to fall in love with a person, we must engage with the person. Thus, reading my words is only meant to help you find your words. The heart of this book is not the five hundred words of reflection but the invitation from Jesus himself to encounter him in the "For Your Prayer" spiritual exercise.

It is easier to know something than it is to love someone. It will also be easier to read this book one day at a time and never engage with the "For Your Prayer" spiritual exercise. But just reading the reflection will, I fear, only help you know something *about* Jesus; it will not dispose you to the grace of knowing him, of falling in love. Therefore, I ask you to let each day's five hundred words of reflection set the stage and draw you into, not away from, the "For Your Prayer" exercise. It is there, in the actual personal prayer, that you will encounter the one whom you desire. And this will require vulnerability, which is why many of us simply read the reflections.

Second, there is a specific reason some "For Your Prayer" exercises are repeated. Some of you have heard me say this before because it is important: In every encounter with God, it is like we are standing at the base of Niagara Falls holding an eight-ounce glass. We may drink all eight ounces, but there is so much more water that could have filled the glass and so much more pouring forth to refill it now. "Repetition" is just a matter of refilling the glass. It is an intentional approach to prayer that St. Ignatius of Loyola describes in his *Spiritual Exercises*.

Repetition, as he defines it, is not an attempt to experience today what I experienced yesterday. Instead, to use the analogy, repetition is merely returning to Niagara Falls with my glass to see if there is more water for me to receive. Throughout this book, many exercises may seem repetitive. This is intentional. Trust the process. More importantly, trust the Lord, who waits for you in the spiritual exercise.

Welcome to Lent. Welcome to an encounter. Welcome to a person, Jesus Christ, who is inviting you to fall in love and stay in love so it decides everything.

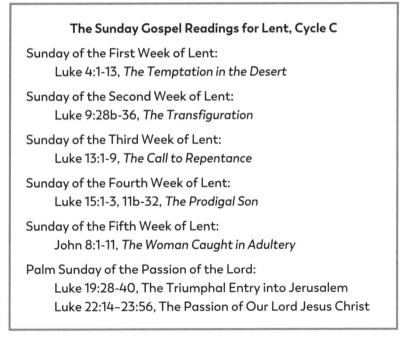

The Sunday Gospel Readings for Lent, Cycle C

Sunday of the First Week of Lent:
Luke 4:1-13, *The Temptation in the Desert*

Sunday of the Second Week of Lent:
Luke 9:28b-36, *The Transfiguration*

Sunday of the Third Week of Lent:
Luke 13:1-9, *The Call to Repentance*

Sunday of the Fourth Week of Lent:
Luke 15:1-3, 11b-32, *The Prodigal Son*

Sunday of the Fifth Week of Lent:
John 8:1-11, *The Woman Caught in Adultery*

Palm Sunday of the Passion of the Lord:
Luke 19:28-40, The Triumphal Entry into Jerusalem
Luke 22:14–23:56, The Passion of Our Lord Jesus Christ

"'Yet even now,' says the LORD,
'return to me with all your heart.'"

—JOEL 2:12

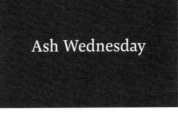

Ash Wednesday

For much of my life, I knew about God. I read lots and lots about the Person without really encountering the reality of the Person. I memorized dogma and amassed cool quotes that could impress listeners. However, interiorly, I lacked a real relationship with the person of Jesus Christ. Many years later, I heard someone say that "it is easier to know something than it is to love someone." This is true. In fact, looking back on my life, I could see that this insight described how I was living. It was safer to know something than it was to love someone.

That was not the case for the very first Christians. The very first believers, the apostles and followers of Jesus Christ, were not Christians because they knew about Jesus. On the contrary, they were Christians because they encountered a person, and that person changed their lives. Take, for example, Peter. The very first words from Jesus to Peter were "Follow me." Look at Matthew. The very first words from Jesus to Matthew were "Follow me." Look at all the apostles. The very first words from Jesus to them were "Follow me."

Follow … *me*. Jesus said, "Follow *me*."

After he had spent every waking moment with them for several years, Jesus looked at his apostles and asked them a piercing question: "Who do the people say that I am?" (Luke 9:18). The question was so important that Jesus eventually reframed it more poignantly: "But who do you say that I am?" (Luke 9:20). Each of us at some point in our life must confront the question and fumble with the truth of the answer: "But who do you say that I am?"

Every year, the Mass readings for Ash Wednesday are the same. So, every year, on the very first day of Lent, at the very first Mass of Lent, the very first words proclaimed from Scripture come to us from the prophet Joel as he writes, "'Yet even now,' says the LORD, 'return to me with all your heart'" (Joel 2:12).

Return ... to *me*.

Notice that the Scriptures do not invite us to return to Lent or return to whatever it is that we have ordinarily done as a Lenten penance. The Scripture says, "Return to *me*." There is a *me* who is calling you. There is a person who is calling you into Lent. The question for you today is, *Who* is it that is calling you?

The only place to start is where you are. God never expects us to be who or where we aren't. Starting where we are requires that we begin by answering his question: "Who do you say that I am?" Who is Jesus? Who is he to you? Where are you in your relationship with him?

If we are to "fall in love in a quite absolute, final way," as Fr. Whelan put it, we will fall in love with a person, a very specific person: Jesus. So, who is he?

He looks at you today and asks you, "Who do you say that I am?"

For Your Prayer

Read Luke 9:18-21. Imagine that Jesus and the apostles are sitting around a campfire. Put yourself in the scene. Imagine you are there with them. Imagine that Jesus looks at you and asks, "Who do you say that I am?"

What words stood out to you as you prayed?
What did you find stirring in your heart?

_____

_____

_____

_____

_____

_____

_____

_____

_____

_____

_____

_____

_____

_____

_____

_____

_____

_____

_____

_____

_____

_____

_____

_____

_____

_____

_____

_____

_____

The Temptation
in the Desert

Human

"And Jesus, full of the Holy Spirit, returned from the Jordan, and was led by the Spirit for forty days in the wilderness."

—LUKE 4:1-2A

Thursday after Ash Wednesday

Nothing threatens the sacred more than familiarity. Let me explain. I have been a priest for more than twenty years. I have celebrated Mass more than twelve thousand times. Every day, I touch sacred chalices, recite sacred words, and perform sacred actions. I would imagine that if you who are reading this book were asked to stand at an altar or touch a chalice and paten or hold in your hands the Precious Body and Blood of our Lord, you would do so with profound reverence and awe. However, I have done that twelve thousand times. With human nature being as it is, it would be understandable if sometimes a person becomes so familiar with the sacred that he loses his experience of awe.

Married couples know this—that nothing threatens the sacred more than familiarity. At first, a man and a woman pay attention to their manners. He opens the door for her. She puts on makeup. They make an effort and try to make a good impression. Then, over time, they grow more familiar with each other. They lose their awe because they stop paying attention. They become too safe and grow too accustomed to their routines. They lose interest in each other.

Nothing threatens the sacred more than familiarity. This is true in our relationship with Jesus. Most of us reading this book are being called to fall in love, not because we are not familiar with Jesus but because we are. We may have become too familiar with Jesus. Jesus may actually feel like an extension of ourselves or someone we have imagined or who we want him to be. This Lent, my prayer is that we rediscover, or, perhaps, discover for the first time, who Jesus really is.

Today, we begin to look ahead to the Gospel that we will encounter in just a few days, on Sunday of the First Week of Lent. There, in Luke 4:1-13, we will read of Jesus' temptation in the desert.[3] There, in the Gospel for this coming Sunday, we are reminded that Jesus, while fully divine, was fully human.

The humanity of Jesus is a remarkable theological reality. The Incarnation happened because God wanted to be known. God wanted us to see his face and hear his voice and feel his touch. Of all the world's religions, Christianity is the only one to boldly proclaim that God has indeed taken on human flesh.

It is precisely because of Jesus' humanity that we are able to fall in love so easily. Every one of us knows what it is like to be in a relationship with a person, and many of us know what it is like to fall in love with a person.

If we are to fall in love, the most natural place to start is with the person, the humanity of Jesus. Let us begin there, in the Gospel for the Sunday of the First Week of Lent, and ask the Lord to reveal the reality of his humanity.

For Your Prayer

Today, read Luke 4:1-13, next Sunday's Gospel reading. Put yourself in the scene. Imagine you are there with Jesus in the desert. Be in the scene. Be there, with him.

What words stood out to you as you prayed?
What did you find stirring in your heart?

_____
_____
_____
_____
_____
_____
_____
_____
_____
_____
_____
_____
_____
_____
_____
_____
_____
_____
_____
_____
_____
_____

Vulnerable

"I was ready to be sought by those who did not ask for me; I was ready to be found by those who did not seek me."

—ISAIAH 65:1

Friday after Ash Wednesday

Jesus was vulnerable. As we slowly unpack the reality of Jesus' humanity, one of the things that may get lost in the details of the Gospel for the Sunday of the First Week of Lent is the reality of Jesus' vulnerability.

To be vulnerable is to be exposed to the possibility of being attacked or harmed, either physically or emotionally. In Luke 4:1-13, we read how Jesus confronts Satan face to face. He faces temptation—he faces evil—in his flesh. Jesus was, in a very real, human way, exposed to the possibility of being attacked or harmed. Furthermore, we read in Luke 4:2, "And he ate nothing in those days; and when they were ended, he was hungry." In his humanity, Jesus was exposed physically in his hunger and in the basic needs of any human being after such dramatic fasting.

The fact that God himself, in the humanity of Jesus Christ, chose to be vulnerable has profound implications for us, now, in this Lent. Just two days ago, on Ash Wednesday, I shared with you that it is easier to know something than it is to love someone. To know something affords me the safety of engaging only with my intellect. But to know someone means choosing to engage all my humanity with the reality of all their humanity. To know someone means to risk the reality of an authentic relationship because vulnerability requires that I expose the truth of who I am with no guarantee of how the other person will receive or respond to my self-revelation.

As I mentioned earlier, it is always easier to know something than it is to love someone. And it is easier to read this book one day at a time without doing the "For Your Prayer" spiritual exercise. Avoiding the prayer exercise will, I fear, only help us know

·

something about Jesus. But it will not dispose us to the grace of knowing him in himself and falling in love. Therefore, I implore you, I beg you, to allow each day's five hundred words of reflection to set the stage and draw you into the "For Your Prayer" spiritual exercise. It is there, in the actual personal prayer, that you will encounter the one whom you desire. However, this will require vulnerability, which is why many of us simply read the reflections.

Please let each day's reflection draw you into "For Your Prayer." Doing so means you will have to become vulnerable too.

Do not be afraid to be vulnerable. Remember that the One you seek in your prayer begins this Lent by revealing his vulnerability to you.

For Your Prayer

Read Luke 4:1-13 again today, as you did yesterday. Put yourself in the scene. Imagine you are there with Jesus in the desert. Be in the scene. Be there, with him.

What words stood out to you as you prayed?
What did you find stirring in your heart?

_____

_____

_____

_____

_____

_____

_____

_____

_____

_____

_____

_____

_____

_____

_____

_____

_____

_____

_____

_____

_____

_____

_____

Needs

"And he ate nothing in those days; and when they were ended, he was hungry."

—LUKE 4:2

As we continue to prepare for the Gospel reading tomorrow, on the first Sunday of Lent, we read carefully in Luke 4:2 that Jesus "ate nothing in those days; and when they were ended, he was hungry." Imagine this for a moment. Jesus was hungry. Jesus had to eat. He had to sleep. He had the same needs we do.

From the very moment of his conception, Jesus had needs. While he was in Mary's womb, Jesus needed her for the nourishment that all unborn children need from their mothers. And, from the very moment of his birth, Jesus needed Mary and Joseph as all infants need their parents—to feed him, keep him clean, hold him, rock him to sleep, and love him. Jesus, in his humanity, had the same basic needs that you and I do.

In these first days of Lent, it is my hope that we rediscover Jesus' humanity. Doing so will dispose us to a deeper relationship and to the grace of falling in love with a very specific person. Few things hasten the deepening of a relationship as much as when someone lets us see their needs. When I reflect on my closest friendships and the people that I truly love, one of the common threads is that I have come to know them at their most vulnerable. When someone chooses to share their needs, they expose their heart in the process. This experience of their heart deepens and matures the relationship in a very real way.

As I pray with Luke 4:1-13, I am moved in my experience of Jesus and his needs. As I place myself in the scene, seeing what Jesus saw, hearing what Jesus heard, feeling what Jesus felt, and sensing his struggles, I experience a new compassion for him as a person. In this experience of him as a person, I find him easier to relate to.

It is almost as if his needs draw me deeper into his heart, and my own heart longs to know him more.

In the experience of praying with this Gospel, I have also come to admit my own needs. I need him. I need mercy. I need love. I don't just want these things; I need these things. And I don't just need to receive them; I need to receive them from a very particular person—from him.

In my prayer, the spiritual exercise of sharing my heart with Jesus has drawn on his vulnerability and my own and has thus been an experience of authentic depth. It is here, in this moment, that I realize that this is what my heart really longs for: depth in my relationship with Jesus.

Jesus is waiting for you. He longs for the depth of an authentic relationship, just as you do. He is inviting you now to be with him in the desert, where his needs are perhaps an entry into his heart.

For Your Prayer

Read Luke 4:1-13 again today. Put yourself in the scene. Imagine you are there with Jesus in the desert. Be in the scene. Be there with him. Ask him to reveal his needs to you. Ask him to take you deeper into his heart.

What words stood out to you as you prayed?
What did you find stirring in your heart?

_____
_____
_____
_____
_____
_____
_____
_____
_____
_____
_____
_____
_____
_____
_____
_____
_____
_____
_____
_____
_____
_____
_____
_____
_____
_____

Dependent

"[Jesus was] tempted by the devil."

—LUKE 4:2

Sunday of the First Week of Lent

As we celebrate the first Sunday of Lent, we read in today's Gospel that Jesus was "tempted by the devil" (Luke 4:2). Furthermore, we read that "he ate nothing in those days; and when they were ended, he was hungry" (Luke 4:2). He was tempted. He was hungry. He was in need. One of the key insights we can glean from Jesus' humanity was that he was forever dependent on the Father for all things.

As I mentioned yesterday, it is my hope that, in these first days of Lent, we will rediscover Jesus' humanity. Why? Yesterday, I mentioned that doing so will dispose us to a deeper relationship and to the grace of falling in love with a very specific person. Today, I would like to share with you my experience of praying with this Gospel for the first Sunday of Lent.

As I placed myself in the scene, I was moved by the fact that Jesus himself was dependent. We know, of course, that Jesus was fully divine. But Jesus himself speaks of his dependence on the Father throughout the Gospels. For example, in John 5:19, he says, "Truly, truly, I say to you, the Son can do nothing of his own accord, but only what he sees the Father doing; for whatever he does, that the Son does likewise."

How is Jesus' dependency helpful for us as we come to know him in a more personal way? As I prayed with today's Gospel, I found Jesus more approachable. He felt like one I could relate to. Let me explain. I have often felt, and perhaps you have too, that Jesus is in a sense untouchable. In the past, in my personal prayer, I knew intellectually that Jesus is fully divine and have tended to compare his perfection to my imperfection. This comparison (which by the way is never of God) made me less confident in approaching him, less confident that he would want to be in a relationship with me.

Yet, in praying with today's Gospel, I felt something different. Jesus felt more approachable. I felt that I could more easily approach him, speak with him, and listen to him. It was precisely because he, just like me, was dependent on the Father that I actually felt more comfortable approaching him.

Here is the good news today. Jesus is waiting for you; he wants you to approach him. He yearns to be in a relationship with you. It is precisely his humanity that gives you permission not to be afraid of your own humanity. Jesus does not want a relationship with you *despite* your imperfections; he wants a relationship with you precisely in your imperfections. Be not afraid. He is approachable.

For Your Prayer

Read John 3:16-17. Put yourself in the scene. It is nighttime. You are with Jesus, a few of his closest disciples, and Nicodemus, who has come in secrecy and fear to meet Jesus. Jesus turns, looks you in the eye, and says these words to you. Be in the scene. Be there, with him. What do you feel? What else do you perceive him to be saying to you today?

What words stood out to you as you prayed?
What did you find stirring in your heart?

_____

_____

_____

_____

_____

_____

_____

_____

_____

_____

_____

_____

_____

_____

_____

_____

_____

_____

_____

_____

_____

_____

_____

_____

_____

_____

Tempted

"The devil said to him ..."

—LUKE 4:3

As we continue to unpack the Gospel for the first Sunday of Lent, we notice the central theme of Jesus being tempted by the devil. Jesus was ... tempted.

Sometimes, I feel as if I am facing temptation, and, sometimes, I feel as if temptation is facing me. What I mean is that in the moments when I am facing temptation, I feel more confident—I can see not only the temptation but also God with me as I experience the temptation. The more quickly I can look to God, the sooner I am usually able to resist the temptation. In those moments, I feel confident because I know God is with me. I feel that I have some control over the outcome, as if I can breathe. And I feel there is hope.

But when I feel as if temptation is facing me, it is as if the devil is right in front of me, staring at me, stealing the very oxygen that I need to breathe. In those moments, I feel seduced by the sin, lured by it. It is as if the temptation is looking at me, and it is the only thing that I can see, the only thing I can focus on. In those moments, I do not look at God because the glare of temptation seems to have blinded me and paralyzed my will, preventing me from seeing anything else. In those moments, I wonder, *What is the point of trying to resist?* I lose confidence. I feel as if the temptation has control over my appetites, as if I can't breathe. And I lose hope.

As I continued to pray with Sunday's Gospel, I felt as if I was right there in the battle. I could feel the devil staring Jesus in the eye. I could feel the cloak of darkness seducing Jesus in his hunger and need. As temptation was facing Jesus, I was stunned with how familiar it felt. Something clicked within me, almost as if to say, "Oh! Jesus knows how I feel, for he too experienced intense temptation."

Yesterday, we saw how Jesus' dependence on the Father made him more approachable. The realization that Jesus truly faced temptation makes him even more approachable—and can be life changing. It is one thing to search for Jesus when we have sinned, to turn to him when we have fallen and are ashamed. It is another thing to search for him in temptation. For some strange reason, it is more familiar for me to ask for God's help when I am in need of mercy and forgiveness than to ask for God's help when I need prudence or temperance or fortitude. How could our lives be different if we began to ask for God's help *during* the temptation, *before* (and we hope instead of) falling into sin?

For Your Prayer

Read Luke 4:3-12. Imagine you are there with Jesus as he faces the devil. Be in the scene. Be there, with him. Notice how Jesus resists temptation. And ask him to speak to you about how you experience temptation and how he can help you when you experience temptation.

What words stood out to you as you prayed?
What did you find stirring in your heart?

_____

_____

_____

_____

_____

_____

_____

_____

_____

_____

_____

_____

_____

_____

_____

_____

_____

_____

_____

_____

_____

_____

_____

_____

_____

_____

_____

Resist

"And Jesus answered him ..."

—LUKE 4:4

Tuesday of the
First Week of Lent

We continue to journey into the Gospel for the Sunday of the First Week of Lent. As we further experience the humanity of Jesus in the midst of temptation, we should notice not just *that* Jesus resisted temptation but also *how* he resisted it.

As I prayed with this Gospel narrative, I was struck with Jesus' responses to the devil. Jesus draws on three quotations from the book of Deuteronomy. Jesus does not try to outwit the devil or pretend the temptation is not real. Jesus does not merely engage his will. He shifts his attention to truths that exist outside the realm of emotion. In the heat of the battle, Jesus goes to the Scriptures.

Why is it so important to go to Scripture? When I struggle with temptation, especially when temptation is facing me instead of me facing temptation, the struggle is often all I can think of. But, when I turn to the Bible for help, several things happen. First, my mind has something else to focus on. Second, the literal words of the Bible help me see God's Word when I cannot hear God's voice. Third, the power of Scripture itself has the authority to cast out evil. So I keep the Scriptures handy, whether in the form of a physical Bible or an app on my phone.

Turning to Scripture in the face of temptation also allows God's words to speak when we do not have the words ourselves. I have often felt the mounting of defeat as temptation lingers too long. The longer I engage with temptation, the less I want to resist. Even when my will does not want to say no, the Word of God often gives me the courage, the ability, and even the very words to use in saying no to temptation and yes to life.

My experience of prayer with the Gospel for the first Sunday of Lent was deeply personal. I felt Jesus say to me, *I want you to succeed more than you want to. I want your holiness more than you want it. I want you to resist temptation more than you want to.* Receiving these words was deeply consoling and actually drew me into his heart.

I pray the same will happen for you. In today's spiritual exercise below, ask the Lord to help you pray. Ask him to take you deeper. Ask him for a personal experience of his presence.

For Your Prayer

Read Luke 4:3-12. Imagine you are there with Jesus as he resists temptation. Be there, with him. Notice how Jesus resists temptation. And ask him to speak to you about how much he longs for your holiness.

What words stood out to you as you prayed?
What did you find stirring in your heart?

_____
_____
_____
_____
_____
_____
_____
_____
_____
_____
_____
_____
_____
_____
_____
_____
_____
_____
_____
_____
_____
_____
_____
_____
_____

Victorious

"And when the devil had ended every temptation, he departed from him."

—LUKE 4:13

Luke 4:13 states, "And when the devil had ended every temptation, he departed from him." The devil loses again, as he will lose every time that he attempts to tempt Jesus. The enemy is defeated. He never wins against Jesus. Never ever.

My entire life, I have known this intellectually; however, something is different as I write these words to you. My experience of prayer with the Gospel for the first Sunday of Lent has affected the way that I see and experience Jesus. I feel even more confident in the One to whom I am praying. I feel even more reassured in his presence, more secure in his strength.

It brings up the question yet again: Who is this person I am coming to know all over again? Who is Jesus? Let us summarize where we have been in these first seven days of Lent. Jesus was a real man, a real human person. He experienced vulnerability. He had needs. He was dependent. He experienced temptation. All of this makes him more approachable, easier to be with, and safer to relate to. However, Jesus, as a real human person, does not live his humanity with the same failings that I do. He was victorious over the devil in the desert. He was victorious over evil then. He is victorious over evil now.

As I concluded my prayer with this week's Gospel, a question pursued me through the quiet moments in the days following. Who was he? Who is he? Who is he to me?

I encourage you to wrestle with the same questions. A week ago, on Ash Wednesday, we began a journey together, and I said, "So who is he?" He looks at you today and asks you directly: "Who do you say that I am?"

You have been with him for seven days. The spiritual exercise below has the same words that you read on Ash Wednesday, but you are not the same as you were then. He is not the same. All that he has blessed you with in this first week is real. All that you have experienced in his humanity is real. Therefore, I beg you today to allow the first seven reflections to set the stage and draw you into today's prayer exercise. It is there, in the actual personal prayer, that you will encounter the One whom you desire.

For Your Prayer

Once again, read Matthew 16:13-15, as you did on Ash Wednesday. Imagine that Jesus and the apostles are sitting around a campfire. Return to the scene. Imagine you are there with them. You belong there. Imagine that Jesus looks you in the eye and asks you to sit next to him. As you come close to him, pay attention to what stirs in you as you sit next to him in all his humanity. Imagine that Jesus looks at you and asks, "Who do you say that I am?" Answer the question from your heart. Then, have the courage to ask, "Who do you say that I am, Lord?" Let him respond. Ask him to reveal how he sees you.

What words stood out to you as you prayed?
What did you find stirring in your heart?

_____
_____
_____
_____
_____
_____
_____
_____
_____
_____
_____
_____
_____
_____
_____
_____
_____
_____
_____
_____
_____
_____
_____
_____

The Transfiguration

Authority

"Master."

—LUKE 9:33

We shift our attention to preparing for the Gospel that awaits us next Sunday, on the Second Sunday of Lent, namely, the story of the Transfiguration. Together, let us ask him to reveal who he really is.

Matter matters. God has given us the sacraments, the Scriptures, sacramentals, and sacred beauty so that he can communicate with us and we can communicate with him. Matter matters.

The physical world communicates spiritual realities. A case in point is the shift in sacred architecture in the mid-twentieth century. Prior to this shift, church architecture intentionally produced objective beauty such as St. Peter's in Rome, Notre Dame in Paris, or the Church of the Holy Sepulchre in Jerusalem. However, we rarely see objectively beautiful churches among those built more recently.

Curious about this phenomenon, I asked why this was. A wise teacher in my life reminded me that with historical sacred architecture, the centrality of the cross, the altar, and the saints intentionally diverted our attention away from ourselves and toward God. He continued with great reverence: "We stopped building churches where God told us who he was, and we started designing churches where we could tell him who we wanted him to be."

Matter matters, and I admit that there are times when I do not want God to reveal who he is so much as I want to tell him who I want him to be.

You are on this journey with me this Lent. I pray that you are able to fall in love with the person of Jesus Christ. But we cannot fall in love with a product of our imagination. We cannot fall in love with a version of Jesus that we want him to be. We can only fall in love with the Jesus who is real, with the Jesus he himself reveals to us.

So, who is Jesus? Well, let us first define who he is not. Jesus is not merely a great man of history, one who lived two thousand years ago. I grieve when I hear or see Jesus portrayed as a historical figure who only taught us to "love one another."

When we reduce Jesus to being just a historical figure, we unknowingly strip him of his authority. Merely historical figures do not have the authority to forgive sins, conquer death, or reconcile man with God. Furthermore, when we treat him this way, we fall victim to thinking that our opinions have the same weight as Jesus' words in Scripture. We think, *Well, the Bible may say this or that, but I'm free to disagree. Jesus will love me anyway.* We have all done this at some point—we have all put our own opinions over God's. So did Adam and Eve. I hope you will have the courage to admit it if you have done this too.

For Your Prayer

Today, read Luke 9:28b-36. Become familiar with the text that we will pray with for the next week. Read the text three times. Let a word or phrase tug at your heart. Sit with this word or phrase today.

What words stood out to you as you prayed?
What did you find stirring in your heart?

_____

_____

_____

_____

_____

_____

_____

_____

_____

_____

_____

_____

_____

_____

_____

_____

_____

_____

_____

_____

_____

_____

_____

_____

Teacher

"Listen to him!"

—LUKE 9:35

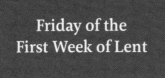

Who is Jesus? This is *the* question this Lent. As we did yesterday, let us define who he is not. The distinctions are more subtle the further we dive into Jesus' identity.

The mounting atheist voice within our secularized culture often depicts Jesus as a wisdom figure, a sage teacher. It often cloaks this as a compliment, highlighting the "essential" teachings of Jesus that are helpful for healthy living. It quotes Jesus as teaching us to "love one another" and to do to others what we would have them do to us (the Golden Rule). However, the false idea here is that Jesus was just *a* teacher. When Jesus is reduced to being just *a* teacher, he is then placed beside other teachers or prophets such as Moses, Mohammad, Confucius, and Gandhi.

Framing Jesus as just *a* wise teacher has implications. First, if someone says Jesus was *merely* a wise teacher, they are actually contradicting his teaching, dismissing the very words they say they value. For Jesus never said he was *just* a teacher. Jesus *himself* referred to himself as God: "Before Abraham was, I am" (John 8:58); "I and the Father are one" (John 10:30); and "He who has seen me has seen the Father" (John 14:9). Jesus' identity as God is at the *core* of his teaching. How can we dismiss his most important teaching and still consider him a "good" teacher?

Second, if Jesus is only *a* teacher, just one among many teachers, then we rob him of his authority as the Son of God. If he has no more authority than any other teacher, we can pick and choose among his teachings, accepting those that appeal to us and ignoring the rest. Third, if Jesus is only *a* teacher, then I can treat Christianity solely as an intellectual exercise, something for my mind but not my heart.

Jesus himself says that *he, and he alone,* has the words of everlasting life. He *is* the Word of everlasting life. Jesus is not *a* teacher. Jesus is *the* teacher. In his own words, Jesus said, "I am the way, *and the truth,* and the life" (John 14:6, emphasis added). As the Word made flesh, Jesus is Truth incarnate, and, as such, every word that he speaks requires our full attention. There is *only one* response to the words of *the* teacher—absolute and unconditional obedience. Furthermore, more than forty thousand of Jesus' words are recorded in the four Gospels. *All* of them, *all* forty thousand, are essential, not merely the fourteen words of the Golden Rule or Jesus' command to love one another.

In Luke 9:35, in the Gospel for the second Sunday of Lent, we read, "And a voice came out of the cloud, saying, 'This is my Son, my Chosen; listen to him!'" The Father wants to get our attention. Jesus is not just *a* teacher; he is *the* teacher. This means the words he speaks to us are more important than any other words. Today, ask for the grace to hear his voice.

For Your Prayer

Today, read Hebrews 4:11-13. Ask Jesus sincerely to open your heart to hear his voice as never before.

What words stood out to you as you prayed?
What did you find stirring in your heart?

Only

"This is my Son, my Chosen."

—LUKE 9:35

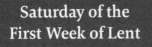

W e begin again today with the question: Who is Jesus? Let us go a little further with noticing first who he is not, and let us pay attention to the subtleties.

However, before we begin, let me comment on an important philosophical shift in Western culture.

In our secular culture, tolerance has become a basic standard for how we behave—replacing ethics and making it difficult, if not impossible, to speak publicly about right and wrong. But morality, ethics, and objective truth are independent of our opinions, personal preferences, and readiness to take offense. In fact, there are clear instances when tolerance can be objectively evil.

Why is this important? Because, at some point, we are confronted with absolutes, with the words Jesus himself said: "Truly, truly, I say to you, *I* am the door of the sheep. ... *I* am the door; if any one enters by *me*, he will be saved" (John 10:7, 9, emphasis added). Jesus is not *a* way to get to heaven, just one among others. Jesus specifically said, *"I* am the way, and the truth, and the life; no one comes to the Father, but by *me*" (John 14:6, emphasis added).

Jesus is not *a* way to get to heaven. Jesus is the *only* way to get to heaven. In our world of tolerance and fear of offending, we may be surprised to hear Jesus say unapologetically that he, and he alone, is the way to salvation. And, if you wonder if Jesus was worried about offending people's sensibilities when he said this, we read just ten verses later that "there was again a division among the Jews because of these words" (John 10:19).

Why is a relationship with Jesus so important? Because he, *and he alone,* is our way to heaven. This reality is not meant to frighten or strong-arm anyone into religion. On the contrary, this reality is the invitation for all of humanity to come to experience God in the flesh: a God who wants to be known on this side of heaven. This reality is not meant to offend or accuse others. It is an invitation to experience objective truth, direction, and salvation in this life and in the life to come. This reality is not meant to aggressively attack other religions, but it is not meant to be hidden either. It is a reality that confronts our fear of saying that if Jesus is right, then others actually may be wrong.

As you and I grow closer to him, I encourage you to ask for a renewed sense of wonder, awe, and respect when we are in his presence. Imagine the awe that Peter, John, and James experienced at the Transfiguration. Do you want that? If so, ask for it. Ask for it today. Ask for a renewed sense of wonder, awe, and respect in Jesus' presence.

For Your Prayer

Read Luke 9:28b-36. Put yourself in the scene.
Imagine you are there with Jesus as one of his closest
followers. Be in the scene. Be there, with him. Imagine
falling to the ground with Peter, James, and John
in awe and wonder at the presence of God.

What words stood out to you as you prayed?
What did you find stirring in your heart?

_____

_____

_____

_____

_____

_____

_____

_____

_____

_____

_____

_____

_____

_____

_____

_____

_____

_____

_____

_____

_____

_____

_____

_____

_____

Reveal

"And as he was praying, the appearance of his countenance was altered, and his clothing became dazzling white."

—LUKE 9:29

I am a passionate dreamer. The Lord has often placed prophetic desires on my heart that I know are from his heart. I do not share those dreams with everyone. When I do reveal them, it is a sign that I both trust and love the other person. Choosing to reveal that part of me reveals something about that person.

When people reveal the truth of who they really are, when they share something deeply personal with you, it reveals something about you too. It shows that they trust you and they love you.

For years, I failed to fully understand or appreciate the significance of the Transfiguration. As I was writing this book, I prayed with Luke 9:29 and was moved with an experience of Jesus at the moment when "his countenance was altered, and his clothing became dazzling white" (Luke 9:29). It felt as if I was there. I felt that I was with Peter, John, and James on top of the mountain. I felt like I was one of those who saw him transfigured.

It was then that it dawned on me: God is revealing something important about himself. In that moment, my experience of Jesus was deeply personal. I could sense that Jesus trusted me and loved me. And he was revealing more than his countenance or his identity. I felt as if he was revealing his heart for me.

There are many theological ways to express the profundity of the Transfiguration. I would like you to consider this: God wants to be known. He is actively and intentionally revealing who he is to all of humanity, including you. In all your searching for God, be reminded that God is searching for you. In all your desire to know him, he is wanting to be known. As you come to know Jesus personally, be reminded that this can only happen because Jesus wants you to know him.

Imagine how it felt for Peter, John, and James to receive such a gift of self-revelation. After all, Jesus did not reveal himself as transfigured to all twelve apostles but only these trusted three. Imagine what it would be like for you if you were in that number, if you were chosen in that way.

For Your Prayer

Read Luke 9:28-29. Put yourself in the scene. Imagine you are there with Jesus as one of his closest followers. Be in the scene. Be there, with him. What does it say about you that Jesus has chosen you to share in this moment of revelation?

What words stood out to you as you prayed?
What did you find stirring in your heart?

_____

_____

_____

_____

_____

_____

_____

_____

_____

_____

_____

_____

_____

_____

_____

_____

_____

_____

_____

_____

_____

_____

Time

"He took with him Peter and John and James."

—LUKE 9:28

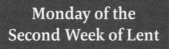

Time is one of those things you never get back. It is, in my opinion, one of the most precious and expensive gifts on the planet. How we use our time shows what is truly valuable to us. Our calendar, you might say, is an objective revelation of our priorities.

On the one hand, time is a powerful conduit of grace. When someone we admire, respect, or love spends time with us, especially if they are truly present to us when they are with us, their time with us is an enormous gift. On the other hand, time, because it is precious, can be painful when it is lost. We will never be able to undo the past. We cannot go back to reclaim the moments we lost from our childhood. Parents cannot reclaim the time they missed with their children. Once our aging, ill, or dying parents are gone, we cannot go back to spend time with them. We cannot go back and spend time with those we neglected.

Time: It is precious.

Imagine the time that Peter had with Jesus. While it was only three years, Peter spent almost every day of those three years, and almost every waking moment of those three years, with Jesus. Much of that time is not recorded in Scripture. Imagine the campfires at night. Imagine what those fraternal conversations must have been like. Imagine the long walks from village to village and all that time on the road. Imagine the personal conversations, spiritual direction, and moments between Jesus and Peter alone.

Imagine all that time. The time they spent together deepened the relationship between Jesus and Peter. Imagine what was given to Peter because of the time he spent with Jesus, and imagine what Peter would never have received if he had missed out on all that time with the Lord.

Time: It is important.

Today, I would like to remind you about the precious gift of time. I do not want to talk about Jesus' time or Peter's time or my time. I want to remind you about your time. Today is Monday of the Second Week of Lent. Today is an ideal moment to commit yourself to spending more time with the Lord. Inevitably, the one thing that will determine how personal Jesus will be in your life this Lent will be your ability to spend time with him alone in prayer.

So, let me ask: How are you doing with the personal prayer and the "For Your Prayer" spiritual exercises? Today is day twelve of Lent. Some of us are spending the time necessary to encounter Jesus in prayer. Great! Keep at it. Some of us started strong and then got distracted. Let us recommit. Some of us have struggled to find the time for personal prayer. If that is you, start fresh today. Wherever we are on the journey, let us all recommit to the time we need for prayer, for it is there that we will fall in love.

For Your Prayer

Read Mark 1:16-35, a typical day in the life of Jesus. Put yourself in the scene. Imagine you are there with Jesus as one of his closest followers. Be in the scene. Be there, with him. Spend time with Jesus on a typical day in his life.

What words stood out to you as you prayed?
What did you find stirring in your heart?

_____
_____
_____
_____
_____
_____
_____
_____
_____
_____
_____
_____
_____
_____
_____
_____
_____
_____
_____
_____
_____
_____
_____
_____
_____

Unafraid

"And as they were coming down the mountain, he charged them to tell no one what they had seen, until the Son of man should have risen from the dead."

—MARK 9:9

As we continue to unpack the Gospel for the Sunday of the Second Week of Lent, I remind you that the Gospel of Luke is not the only account of the Transfiguration. The Gospels of Matthew and Mark both have similar accounts of the Transfiguration. In Mark 9:9 we read, "And as they were coming down the mountain, he charged them to tell no one what they had seen, until the Son of man should have risen from the dead."

Peter wanted to stay on the mountaintop. "Peter said to Jesus, 'Master, it is well that we are here; let us make three booths, one for you and one for Moses and one for Elijah'" (Luke 9:33). I would want the same thing. I would want to stay up there where things were glorious. But Jesus is more than a mere human. He is God, and he is unafraid. While the Bible does not include these words, we might imagine Jesus confidently saying something like this to his disciple: "Peter, I'm going down the mountain. If you stay up here, you will be alone again. Going down the mountain means I have to face pain, suffering, and death. But I choose to leave this place and go down there, for I am unafraid of what awaits."

As we continue to ask ourselves about Jesus, about this person we are coming to fall in love with, one thing that we relearn from the Transfiguration is that Jesus was unafraid. In the desert, Jesus was unafraid of the devil. In the Garden of Gethsemane, Jesus, while fully aware of the immense suffering that awaited him, was unafraid of his passion. Jesus was unafraid, and Jesus is still unafraid.

Jesus is unafraid of your messiness and sin. Jesus is unafraid of your inconsistency and habit of running away. Jesus is unafraid of your questions and doubts. Regardless of what you are afraid of and how often you experience your fear, Jesus remains unafraid.

This reality can be immensely helpful as you are getting to know Jesus in a more personal way. Why? Because it is one thing for Jesus to call us, but it is another thing for us to follow him and to do so permanently. I wonder how many times Peter, Matthew, or Mary Magdalene were afraid and wanted to walk away. I wonder how many times the apostles heard Jesus speak of his death only to then grow afraid and consider leaving. After all, only one of the apostles, John, made it to the foot of the Cross. And, even after they knew of his resurrection, we read that "on the evening of that day, the first day of the week, the doors [were] shut where the disciples were, for fear of the Jews" (John 20:19).

When I am afraid, I take great comfort in knowing that Jesus is not. Be with him, for he is calling you, and he is not afraid.

For Your Prayer

Today, read Luke 8:26-33. Put yourself in the scene. Imagine you are there with Jesus as he confronts evil. Be in the scene. Be there, with him. Experience his authority and confidence. Ask Jesus to help you experience what it is like for him to be unafraid.

What words stood out to you as you prayed?
What did you find stirring in your heart?

_____

_____

_____

_____

_____

_____

_____

_____

_____

_____

_____

_____

_____

_____

_____

_____

_____

_____

_____

_____

_____

_____

_____

_____

_____

Deeper

"*Therefore let us leave the elementary doctrines of Christ and go on to maturity.*"

—HEBREWS 6:1

Wednesday of the Second Week of Lent

Today marks two weeks. It has been exactly two weeks since Ash Wednesday, two weeks since we began a journey this Lent. These two weeks have laid a foundation so that we might know who it is that we are called to fall in love with.

In our first week, we experienced his humanity. I reminded you last Wednesday that Jesus was a real man, a real human person. He experienced vulnerability. He had needs. He was dependent. He experienced temptation. All of this makes him more approachable, easier to be with, and safer to relate to. In our second week, we experienced his divinity. We talked about who he is not. He is not merely a historical figure or *a* teacher or *a* way to get to heaven. He is God—*the* teacher and *the* way to heaven—as the Transfiguration clearly reveals. There, he is glorified on the top of the mountain, and he is unafraid to confront the suffering that awaits him when he goes back down.

In these first two weeks, you have come to know him. And yet, there is more; he is calling you to go deeper. I once heard it said that Jesus loves us enough to meet us exactly where we are, but he loves us too much to leave us there. There is always more.

Day after day, in the "For Your Prayer" spiritual exercise, I have been encouraging you to enter into a Gospel passage. I pray that you are investing this time in your personal prayer and growing in your ability to be with Jesus' most trusted friends. Today, let us imagine what it must have been like for Peter, John, and James. Jesus was always calling them deeper too. We can imagine that, just when they thought they had things down, when they thought they had their lives with him figured out, Jesus called them deeper.

Because Jesus himself is an inexhaustible well of mercy, love, and freedom, there is always more. We can always go deeper.

As I mentioned earlier, in the introduction, every encounter with God is like standing at the base of Niagara Falls with an eight-ounce glass. No matter how much we drink, there is always more.

Today, I would like you to return yet again to Matthew 16, as you did on Ash Wednesday, and again a week ago. Trust the process of returning to this passage, for it is the theme of this Lent. Be there again. Hear the question anew.

For Your Prayer

Once again, read Matthew 16:13-15. Imagine that Jesus and the apostles are sitting around a campfire. Return to the scene. Imagine you are there with them. You belong there. Imagine that Jesus looks you in the eye and asks you to sit next to him. As you come close to him, pay attention to what stirs within as you sit next to him in all his humanity. Imagine that Jesus looks at you and asks, "Who do you say that I am?" Answer the question from your heart. Then, have the courage to ask, "Who do you say that I am, Lord?" Let him respond. Ask him to reveal how he sees you.

What words stood out to you as you prayed?
What did you find stirring in your heart?

_____
_____
_____
_____
_____
_____
_____
_____
_____
_____
_____
_____
_____
_____
_____
_____
_____
_____
_____
_____
_____
_____
_____
_____
_____
_____
_____

The Call
to Repentance

Person

"*Unless you repent
you will all likewise perish.*"

—LUKE 13:5

For much of my life, there was a person at the center of my life, and that person was me. Even my spiritual life was about me. Prayer was about me, insofar as so much of what I said to God was about things I really wanted, even if they were not what I really needed. What I wanted in prayer was about me. If I felt consolation from God in prayer, it made me feel good. If I did not, then I was disappointed, not because of the relationship but because I did not feel the feelings. Narcissism has its tentacles in most of us, and, for a long time, much of my spiritual life was just a different face of my narcissism.

An antidote for narcissism in our spiritual lives is to become fascinated with something other than ourselves. The more we allow ourselves to encounter another person, the more we can hope to become absorbed in them and not in ourselves.

Today, we shift our attention to preparing for the Gospel that awaits us on the third Sunday of Lent, namely, the call to repentance. Jesus uses the example of two tragedies—Pilate's murder of some Galileans and the death of others in the collapse of a tower—to call us to repentance. It wasn't their sin that directly caused these worldly disasters, but if we choose to refuse repentance, something worse will happen to us. He then tells the parable of the barren fig tree, showing us that he has given us time to turn back to him, but the time is short. We need to repent, and we need to repent today.

Our emphasis in the remaining weeks of Lent will be on seeing Jesus as he really is and on seeing ourselves as Jesus really sees us. What we look at, what captures our attention, and how we see ourselves are perhaps three of the most influential dynamics of our spiritual lives. Most important are how we see Jesus, how we see ourselves, and how we experience being seen by him.

There are several versions of the act of contrition—the prayer that we say during confession to express sorrow for our sins. However, let us allow the words of the traditional version to teach us about repentance today:

> O my God, I am heartily sorry for having offended you and I detest all my sins, because I dread the loss of heaven and the pains of hell, but most of all because I have offended you, my God, who are all good and deserving of all my love.
>
> I firmly resolve with the help of your grace, to confess my sins, to do penance and to amend my life. Amen.

Notice the words "But most of all because I have offended you, my God." Most of all—I repeat it: most of all—it is because I have hurt someone other than me. This is the grace we pray for this week, that we might grow in our experience of the Lord.

For Your Prayer

Today, pray with the words of the act of contrition above. Read it three times, each time very slowly. Pick a word or phrase that tugs at your heart, and ponder it throughout the day.

What words stood out to you as you prayed?
What did you find stirring in your heart?

_____

_____

_____

_____

_____

_____

_____

_____

_____

_____

_____

_____

_____

_____

_____

_____

_____

_____

_____

_____

_____

_____

_____

_____

Look

*"But my eyes are toward you, O L*ORD *God;*
in you I seek refuge;
leave me not defenseless!"

—PSALM 141:8

Friday of the
Second Week of Lent

As we prepare for the third Sunday of Lent, our attention shifted yesterday to Luke 13:1-9, which the Church has selected to be read during Lent because of its emphasis on repentance. Like the barren fig tree, the Lord has given us time to bear fruit, but the time is short. At the heart of repentance is conversion. But what does the word *conversion* mean? The Latin word *convertere* means "to turn around" or, more relationally, "to turn toward."

We are meant to live our lives looking into the eyes of the Lord. But we often turn away, casting our gaze onto someone or something that has captured our attention. While writing that sentence, I was stopped in my tracks. I began to pray and ask the Lord for insight. What he revealed is that I have never sinned when my eyes are fixed intently on him. Never. Ever. It is only when I look away that I sin. Something precedes the action of sin, for first I stop looking at God. Therefore, it makes sense that conversion requires that I "relook" at the One I stopped looking toward. In other words, where the eyes go, the heart follows. When the eyes stray from the Lord, so does the heart. And when the eyes return to the Lord, so does the heart.

Returning to my experience of prayer above, I was further surprised when the Lord revealed that it is not only the discipline of looking again at him that is important but also my desire to look at him. In other words, over the course of our lives we build up an affection for sin. We become desensitized to the evil in it, and we actually begin to crave the temporary false satisfaction that accompanies any of the seven deadly sins. The question I perceived from Jesus was this: Do I long for him as much as I am tempted toward my go-to sins?

There is something about looking into the eyes of a person that has an effect on us. It is one thing for us to send text messages or even speak to someone on the phone. But things change when we can see another's eyes. The other person can say the same words as they would send in a text message or speak over the phone, but when we see them while hearing them, those words feel different.

The art of looking at Jesus, looking at him again after we have turned away, and keeping our gaze on him in temptation is perhaps at the heart of our spiritual lives. Even deeper than that is the invitation to yearn for his gaze. When we long to see him and long to be with him, over time the temporary satisfaction temptation offers us will fail in comparison to what we experience when we are with Jesus.

For Your Prayer

Again today, pray with the words of the act of contrition. Read it three times, each time reading it very slowly. Pick a word or phrase that tugs at your heart, and ponder it throughout the day.

What words stood out to you as you prayed?
What did you find stirring in your heart?

_____
_____
_____
_____
_____
_____
_____
_____
_____
_____
_____
_____
_____
_____
_____
_____
_____
_____
_____
_____
_____
_____
_____
_____
_____
_____
_____
_____
_____

Seen

*"Because you are precious in my eyes,
and honored, and I love you."*

—ISAIAH 43:4

I learned how to hide when I was a kid, and I am not talking about the fun of hide and seek. Unfortunately, I am speaking of hiding from, and because of, our mistakes. Desperate for attention, validation, and affirmation, I learned early in life that if I hid my mistakes, I would not have to suffer the public humiliation of failure. In an unhealthy way, I actually became quite good at hiding. This eventually invaded my relationships. I would hide my failures from God, from people, and, through denial, even from myself. I hid as Adam and Eve hid from God.

Yesterday, we highlighted the importance of turning and looking at God again whenever we have taken our gaze away from him. That is the first part. But, once we have looked again at Jesus, we also have to let ourselves be seen. The gardener tenderly and carefully examines the barren fig tree. What does it need? Where is it unhealthy? How can I give nurture and healing? To let ourselves be seen—to let ourselves be seen in this tender, thorough examination from God—can be much harder to do.

Most of us know how vulnerable we can feel in being seen, especially in our sin. For example, many of us have experienced difficult conversations when we did not want to look the other person in the eye. Our fear of being seen comes out in other ways as well. It is often apparent in the way that we practice the sacrament of Reconciliation.

How many times have I sinned and then felt prompted to go to confession immediately within the sacrament of Reconciliation? However, there was a point in my life when I would not do so immediately. Instead, I would wait, rationalizing convenient "excuses" for why I should not or could not go right away. I would go eventually but not immediately. Why? Because the longer I waited, the further I distanced myself from the immediacy of the shame. Once I had distanced myself from the feelings associated with failure, I felt less vulnerable in being seen by God.

There is no clearer example of the fear of being seen than resisting the sacrament of Reconciliation altogether. Sometimes, we rationalize it intellectually, coming up with reasons why we don't have to go. However, in the end—and I say this with great love—there is only one reason *really* why people don't go to confession: It is because we all have a fear of being seen. Of course, most of us are unaware of this, and so we cling to reasons we have made up about why we don't have to go. But really, in the end, if we are brutally honest, our arguments are flimsy. In the end, it all boils down to fear. We are afraid of being looked at.

Part of falling in love with Jesus is letting him look at us. But we have to choose to let ourselves be looked at. We have to choose to let ourselves be seen. Today's "For Your Prayer" is important. Ask for the grace to be seen.

For Your Prayer

Imagine that it is the end of a long day in Jesus' life. You are there with him by a campfire. In the stillness of the night, Jesus turns and looks at you. He looks you deeply in the eyes. There is silence, only silence. Stay still, and let yourself be seen.

What words stood out to you as you prayed?
What did you find stirring in your heart?

Lens

"*For the* L ORD *sees not as man sees.*"

—1 SAMUEL 16:7

Sunday of the Third Week of Lent

One of my favorite writings from Pope Benedict XVI is *God Is Love*. The encyclical is rich in wisdom. The Holy Father writes:

> Love of neighbour is thus shown to be possible in the way proclaimed by the Bible, by Jesus. It consists in the very fact that, in God and with God, I love even the person whom I do not like or even know. This can only take place on the basis of an intimate encounter with God, an encounter which has become a communion of will, even affecting my feelings. Then I learn to look on this other person not simply with my eyes and my feelings, but from the perspective of Jesus Christ. ... Seeing with the eyes of Christ, I can give to others much more than their outward necessities; I can give them the look of love which they crave.[4]

Pope Benedict connects loving with seeing and being loved with being seen. Unfortunately, most of us do not see correctly. Most of us see others through our eyes, through our lens.

It is the way we see that prevents us from loving well. This is what the Holy Father refers to when he says, "I learn to look on this other person not simply with my eyes and my feelings, but from the perspective of Jesus Christ."

I have worn glasses most of my life. My eyes do not take in reality the way they should. Thus, the lenses of my glasses help me see reality as it is. Those lenses, through which I see the world, have a great influence.

Likewise, you and I look at God, others, and ourselves through our own damaged lens. This lens has been affected by all our experiences: our pain and joy, regrets and gratitude, and, specifically, our judgments about life, others, and ourselves. We do not perceive reality as it is; rather, we see life through a lens that distorts reality.

As you and I fall in love with Jesus, we are met with his desire to see us. But we must let ourselves be seen. What complicates this is the lens through which we see ourselves and God. This is why it is difficult for many of us to be seen, because we see ourselves through our own lens of judgment, and we assume that Jesus sees us the same way. We sometimes think like the crowd speaking to Jesus in today's Gospel, as if saying, "If God sees me in my sin, he will immediately smite me down, the tower will fall in on me, or something else bad will happen."

The good news that we will unpack over the next few days is that God sees you only through the lens of love. He is not vindictive. He is not petty. He only desires to welcome you into his love. For now, trust the process. Focus on the spiritual exercise below.

For Your Prayer

Return to the campfire. Imagine again that it is the end of a long day in Jesus' life. You are there with him by the campfire. It is just you and Jesus, no one else. In the stillness of the night, Jesus turns and looks at you. He looks you deeply in the eyes. There is silence, only silence. Stay still, and let yourself be seen. If at any point it feels awkward, or if at any point you feel that you want to turn away from his gaze, ask him for help. Remember, he does not look at you through your lens; he has his own lens of pure love.

What words stood out to you as you prayed?
What did you find stirring in your heart?

Past

"But one thing I do, forgetting what lies behind and straining forward to what lies ahead."

—PHILIPPIANS 3:13

Monday of the Third Week of Lent

Yesterday, we talked about how many of us see ourselves, others, and God through a lens. I mentioned yesterday that this lens is composed of all the experiences of our lives: our pain and joy, regrets and gratitude, and, specifically, our judgments about life, others, and ourselves. Thus, we do not perceive reality as it is. Rather, we see life through our own damaging and distorting lens.

One of the most powerful distortions comes from our past. Life is not perfect, and none of us has had a perfect past. With each trial, suffering, and failure, we tend to come up with interpretations about why it happened, what it means about us, and what it implies about God. We form judgments, especially about ourselves, and these judgments distort the lens through which we see ourselves, and they affect how we imagine other people see us too.

We may be tempted to see ourselves as a sum of our failures. As in the parable of the barren fig tree, we may be tempted to focus only on the years of fruitlessness, desolation, and difficulty. When this happens, we amass all our sins and failings together in such a way that we do not see ourselves *through* the failure but *as* a failure. This is an unfortunate attack on our heart. The failure ceases to be about an event and now claims our very identity.

One of the reasons many of us struggle to fall in love and stay in love with Jesus is this difficulty in letting ourselves be seen by him. It may be because we see ourselves through the sum of our failures or because of what we think of ourselves in light of our failures, pain, and suffering. We assume that Jesus sees us the same way.

As I mentioned yesterday, the good news is that God sees us only through the lens of love. Again, trust the process. Give yourself the time necessary for the spiritual exercise below.

For Your Prayer

Return to the campfire. As you did yesterday, imagine that it is the end of a long day in Jesus' life. You are there with him by the campfire. It is just you and Jesus, no one else. In the stillness of the night, Jesus turns and looks at you. He looks you deeply in the eyes. Stay still, and let yourself be seen.

Now imagine that Jesus looks at you and asks, "Who do you say that I am?" Answer the question from your heart. Then, have the courage to ask, "Who do you say that I am, Lord?" Let him respond. Ask him to reveal how he sees you.

As before, if at any point it feels awkward, or if you want to turn away from his gaze, ask him for help. Remember, he does not look at you through your lens. He has his own lens of pure love.

What words stood out to you as you prayed?
What did you find stirring in your heart?

_____

_____

_____

_____

_____

_____

_____

_____

_____

_____

_____

_____

_____

_____

_____

_____

_____

_____

_____

_____

_____

_____

_____

_____

Love

"God is love."

—1 JOHN 4:8

Tuesday of the Third Week of Lent

I would like to return to what Pope Benedict XVI wrote in *Deus Caritas Est*. But I am going to paraphrase it this time to make the same truth more personal. The Holy Father is writing about the love of neighbor, but what he says also applies to our love for ourselves:

> Love of [ourselves] is thus shown to be possible in the way proclaimed by the Bible, by Jesus. It consists in the very fact that, in God and with God, I love even [the parts of me that] I do not like or even know. This can only take place on the basis of an intimate encounter with God, an encounter which has become a communion of will, even affecting my feelings. Then, I learn to look at [myself] not simply [through my lens], but from the perspective of Jesus Christ. ... Seeing with the eyes of Christ, I can [receive] much more than [my] outward necessities; I can [receive] the look of love which [I] crave."

Jesus does not see you the way you see yourself. Jesus sees you through the lens of love because Jesus *is* love. Love is not something Jesus does; love is who Jesus *is*. He is pure love, and, thus, he sees us without our distorting lens or the judgments that cloak us with a false identity. Jesus sees us as we are, as we always have been in his eyes.

Even though you may not feel it, please know that I am praying for you. Every morning, as I pray the Morning Prayer in the Liturgy of the Hours, I include a special intention for you who are reading this book as part of your Lenten experience. As I pray for you, I ask the Lord to give you all that you desire and so much more. I pray that you are encountering the person of Jesus Christ and falling in love in a whole new way.

Please know that today I am praying for you and your experience of the spiritual exercise below. Today's personal prayer is important. Be sure to carve out time for this prayer.

For Your Prayer

Read Luke 7:36-50. Imagine you are there with Jesus as the sinful woman approaches him. Imagine that you are with Jesus, right next to him. Notice how Jesus looks at her. Regardless of how she sees herself, Jesus sees her with mercy and compassion. The lens through which he sees her is pure love. Watch the scene unfold.

Now imagine that it is later, at the end of this same day in Jesus' life. Once again, you are there with him by the campfire. It is just you and Jesus, no one else. Again, in the stillness of the night, Jesus turns and looks at you. He looks you deeply in the eyes.

Ask him to reveal to you any ways that your past or any part of your past has affected the way you see yourself, life, others, or God. And ask him to show you what he sees (not what you see) when he looks at your past. Trust him. Trust the way he sees you, for he is pure love.

What words stood out to you as you prayed?
What did you find stirring in your heart?

_____

_____

_____

_____

_____

_____

_____

_____

_____

_____

_____

_____

_____

_____

_____

_____

_____

_____

_____

_____

_____

_____

_____

_____

_____

Repetition

"And the Word became flesh and dwelt among us,
full of grace and truth; we have beheld his glory,
glory as of the only-begotten Son from the Father."

—JOHN 1:14

As we wrap up our unpacking of the Gospel for the third Sunday of Lent, let us summarize where we have been. The core message of these past seven days has been on how Jesus sees us as compared with how we see ourselves. To grow in ongoing conversion means we mature in our ability to turn back toward Jesus after we have turned away. We must let ourselves be seen. What often prevents us from being seen by Jesus is a fear based on how we see ourselves. Each of us has a lens through which we see ourselves and the world. This lens comprises our pain and joy, our regrets and gratitude, and, specifically, our judgments about life, others, and ourselves. We may even see ourselves as a sum of our failures. Worse yet, we may assume that this is also how Jesus sees us.

The good news proclaimed to us this week is that Jesus sees us through the eyes of love, for Jesus is love. Love is not what Jesus does; love is who Jesus is. To grow in our relationship with him, asking for the grace to fall in love with him, we learn to see ourselves as Jesus sees us. This grace liberates our heart and further disposes us to receive more of his love as well as the love of others.

Our meditations this past week were built on the foundation of the first two weeks. We began with Jesus' humanity, where he is more like us, more approachable, easier to be with, and safer to relate to. We then moved on to reflect on his divinity as revealed in the Transfiguration. A balanced understanding of the real Jesus—100 percent God and 100 percent human—allows us to understand the truth of how he sees us and hear the call to repentance as an invitation to freedom.

Today is Wednesday, and, on this Wednesday, I would like to bring us back to what I wrote earlier, in the introduction. First, remember that it is easier to know something than it is to love someone. Reading about the things we have looked at in these weeks will help us, but *experiencing* them will transform us.

As with the earlier Wednesdays this Lent, I would like you to return again to Matthew 16. Trust the process of repetition, which I also talked about in the introduction. This passage is important, for it is the theme of this Lent. Be there again in the scene it sets, and hear the questions anew.

For Your Prayer

Once again, read Matthew 16:13-15. Imagine that Jesus and the apostles are sitting around the campfire. Return to the scene. Imagine you are there with them. You belong there. Imagine that Jesus looks you in the eye and asks you to sit next to him. As you come close to him, pay attention to what stirs within as you sit next to him. Imagine that Jesus looks at you and asks, "Who do you say that I am?" Answer the question from your heart. Then, have the courage to ask, "Who do you say that I am, Lord?" Let him respond. Ask him to reveal how he sees you.

What words stood out to you as you prayed?
What did you find stirring in your heart?

_____

_____

_____

_____

_____

_____

_____

_____

_____

_____

_____

_____

_____

_____

_____

_____

_____

_____

_____

_____

_____

_____

The Prodigal Son

Face

"I will arise and go to my father."

—LUKE 15:18

Thursday of the
Third Week of Lent

Love is better thought of as a verb than as a noun. The human person is meant to experience life through all their senses, but love is more than emotion, attraction, or desire. Inevitably, love is fully revealed in what we do. You might say that the fullness is in how we act on love, not in how we feel love.

I know this to be true. There have been many people in my life who have revealed love to me. My mother is a quiet saint. Her sacrifice, consistency, and quiet virtue were necessary for me to learn to love others, as well as the foundation of my relationship with the Blessed Mother. My father is also one of my heroes. There have been many moments in my life when he has revealed love as a verb, but one of those moments will forever be a part of my memory.

After I graduated from college, I ventured off to Washington, DC, a little like the younger son of Luke 15 as he wandered off with his inheritance. Oddly enough, it was there in Washington, DC, during the darkest time in my spiritual life, that God spoke loudly, calling me to the seminary. To enter the seminary, though, I needed to take care of personal things that required me to ask my father for help. I needed to have a face-to-face conversation with him. And I remember the conversation distinctly. His response was merciful and loving, and I shall never forget that. But I also remember how important it was for me to face my father. I will never forget what it was like to have to face him in person.

Today, we shift our attention to the Gospel that awaits us on the fourth Sunday of Lent: Luke 15:1-3, 11-32, the parable of the Prodigal Son. I assume that you are familiar with the story of the Prodigal Son, for it is the most popular story in the entire New Testament. It tells about the wayward son who "gathered all he had and took his journey into a far country, and there he squandered his property in loose living" (Luke 15:13). Soon, coming to his senses, he said to himself, "How many of my father's hired servants have bread enough and to spare, but I perish here with hunger! I will arise and go to my father" to beg for mercy (Luke 15:17-18).

The son had sinned against his father; he had sinned against a very particular person. And he knew that to truly restore the relationship, he had to face his father. He could not reconcile impersonally. It had to happen face to face.

For Your Prayer

Today, read Luke 15:1-3 and 11-32. Read it slowly. Take your time. Once you have read the passage, close your eyes and enter the scene. You are the son. You must return home to your father, which of course is an image for God. You must return to face Jesus, to look him in the eye. Take your time, be in the scene, and ask the Lord to guide you as you pray.

What words stood out to you as you prayed?
What did you find stirring in your heart?

Shame

"So he got up and went back."

—LUKE 15:20 (NAB)

L et us continue to prepare for Sunday's Gospel as we imagine what the journey home must have been like for the Prodigal Son. Today, I would like to shift a little by inviting you into a guided meditation. This is based on the Gospel story but will include details that are not found there.

Let us imagine that the Prodigal Son has been away for months now, and the wreckage of his sin has caught up with him. He has squandered all the money he left home with. For the last two months, he has hired himself out to a farmer. Day after day he feeds swine, the filthiest of all animals. He has not eaten in two days. He has not bathed in two months. The problem with this is not just that he smells abhorrent; it is that he has become so accustomed to the stench that he no longer notices it.

Last night, he fell asleep with the very swine he tends to. As he wakes this morning, he struggles to lift his head. His hair, matted in mud and filth, is stuck to the very mud that he is sleeping in. As he struggles to free his hair from the mud, he straightens himself in horror. He sees swine relieving themselves in the very mud he lies in. Caked in filth and disgusted with himself, he is soon racked with hunger pains and bent over in affliction.

This is it. He has had enough. If there is such a thing as rock bottom, this is it. He says to himself, "How many of my father's hired servants have bread enough and to spare, but I perish here with hunger! I will arise and go to my father, and I will say to him, 'Father, I have sinned against heaven and before you; I am no longer worthy to be called your son; treat me as one of your hired servants'" (Luke 15:17-19). As soon as those words leave his mouth he begins to weep. The words "treat me as one of your hired servants" means to beg his father to be a slave. In an instant, he is filled with shame. Tears pour forth uncontrollably.

The return home will take him at least a month, maybe more. He will need to beg as he travels. But his stench and filth are so repulsive that even the most charitable of pilgrims is likely to avoid him.

As he walks home, he is tormented by the voices of fear and accusation within him. His imagination is getting the best of him as he begins to think about what will happen when he arrives home. What will his brother say? What will the villagers think? He imagines the shame of living as a slave, even in his father's house.

And then, there is his father. He will have to face his father. He will have to look his father in the eye. With every step he is gripped with fear of what will happen. Every step home is marred with shame.

For Your Prayer

Today, close your eyes and visualize the son as he walks toward home, putting yourself in his place. Imagine yourself in the scene above. Invest the time needed today for your personal prayer.

What words stood out to you as you prayed?
What did you find stirring in your heart?

Waiting

"While he was yet at a distance,
his father saw him."

—LUKE 15:20

We continue to prepare for tomorrow's Gospel reading as we dive deeper into the story of the Prodigal Son. Yesterday gave us an opportunity to imagine what it must have been like for the wayward son to travel home. We can only imagine how he imagined the worst. The son feared facing his father so much that he was prepared to live the rest of his life as a slave. Furthermore, we can only imagine how this son feared his brother, knowing his brother to be righteous but also judgmental and rigid. With every step closer to home, the Prodigal Son was visualizing his worst fears coming true.

Now that we have the Prodigal Son situated in the story, let us consider what may have been happening in the heart of the father. Luke 15:20 states that "while [the son] was yet at a distance, his father saw him." Let us pause to savor this life-changing insight. It is the father who sees the son first. How can this be? Well, two thousand years ago, travel often meant walking what we would consider long distances. It was common back then for travelers to walk during the morning hours, before the sun rose, and then to rest during the hotter hours. Then, in the later afternoon and early evening, when the sun was cooler, travelers would resume their walking. Therefore, the father knew that if his son were to return, it would be late in the morning or early in the evening.

The fact that his father saw him "while he was yet at a distance" means that the father must have been watching for his son's return. How extraordinary! It was the father who longed for his son's return!

The story of the Prodigal Son is a parable. It is meant to communicate a message. Jesus was intentionally telling the story to reveal the mercy and compassion that is his Sacred Heart. This Jesus, this person with whom we are falling in love—this is the kind of heart he has. It is a heart of mercy. It is a heart of pure love.

Contrast what was in the mind of the son as he walked home with what was in the mind of the father. The son feared facing his father, while the father was longing for him every day, hoping that this would be the day he would see his son.

For Your Prayer

Today, close your eyes and imagine that Jesus is waiting day after day for the return of the Prodigal Son. Imagine Jesus on the edge of a vast piece of property, standing in the center of the road by its entrance.

Imagine that you are there with Jesus. You are there, in the scene. Be in the scene, next to Jesus. Stand there and wait with Jesus. As you pray, imagine that Jesus turns his head for a moment and looks you in the eye. Notice what is in his eyes. What is in his heart? Ask Jesus to reveal his heart to you as it is in the story of the Prodigal Son.

What words stood out to you as you prayed?
What did you find stirring in your heart?

Ran

"His father saw him ...
and ran and embraced him."

—LUKE 15:20

Let us continue to enter into the Gospel for this fourth Sunday of Lent as we are drawn into the father's act of running toward his son. Luke 15:20 says, "His father saw him ... and ran."

Why would he run? There is no explanation of this detail in Luke 15. But we can consider three possible reasons why anyone, especially this father, would run toward their son. They are, first, anticipation; second, urgency; and third, grief. Let us unpack these one at a time.

Anticipation. The father may have run toward his son because he wanted to. Day after day, he waited at the edge of his property hoping that this would be the day his son would return. Every day, he went to look. Every day, he waited. Every day, he returned home hoping that tomorrow would be the day. We can only imagine what an explosion of joy erupted in his heart on the day that he finally saw his son. It is easy to imagine the father running to his son because of anticipation.

Urgency. The father may have run toward his son because he was compelled to. Day after day, the father waited, knowing full well that the son's soul was in danger. It was not just that his son stank and was financially bankrupt, for those things can be remedied. The father was deeply concerned about his son's soul. The danger of the darkness that tormented his son was a darkness that the father felt. Thus, the father ran to his son out of a sense of urgency.

Grief. The father may have run toward his son in grief. Only a parent can imagine the love that a father has for his own flesh and blood. The father had been grieving from the very moment the son asked for his inheritance. Remember how the father later said to the older son, "All that is mine is yours" (Luke 15:31). The same was always true for the younger son as well. Since his son left, the father's heart has ached with grief for the young man's misery and sin. And now, as the father sees his son again, he runs to him in grief.

All of this is true of Jesus. This is Jesus, whom you are coming to know and love. His heart is filled with anticipation for you. No matter how unworthy you feel, he brims with the anticipation of love, the delight of giving himself to you. He is also passionately concerned about your soul and your eternal salvation. Even when you are not concerned about salvation, he is. There is an urgency in his heart for your soul. There is also grief in his heart for the darkness you have experienced, for your suffering and sin.

For Your Prayer

Today, close your eyes and imagine that Jesus is waiting day after day for the return of the Prodigal Son. Imagine that you are there with Jesus. You are there, in the scene. Be in the scene, next to Jesus. All of a sudden, he catches a glimpse of his son in the distance.

Jesus looks you in the eye just before he runs to his son. What is in his heart? Ask Jesus to reveal his heart to you as it is in the story of the Prodigal Son. Then, run with him as he runs toward the son.

What words stood out to you as you prayed?
What did you find stirring in your heart?

Compassion

"His father saw him and had compassion."

—LUKE 15:20

Luke 15:20 tells us more about the story of the Prodigal Son, as we read, "His father saw him and had compassion ... and kissed him" (Luke 15:20). The word *compassion* literally means "feeling of sorrow or deep tenderness for one who is suffering or experiencing misfortune." The prefix *com-* means "with or together," and *-pati* means "to suffer" (as in passion). *Compassion* means to suffer with someone. In fact, the greatest expression of compassion may be to suffer *for* someone.

The father had compassion for his son. The father was overcome with "deep tenderness" for his son who was suffering. As the son walked home, he was playing out in his imagination what he thought would happen when he returned. Day after day, step after step, he imagined all his fears panning out, the worst of all having to face his father and beg to be a slave. Imagine the assault of shame that must have gripped the son when he thought his father would make him a slave. It would be like the father saying, "You are dead to me. Dead. Gone. You are not my son; you are only a slave."

With every step the son imagined all his worst fears coming to fruition. Now, with *that* as the backdrop, imagine what would have been in his heart when he saw his father running toward him. He must have been shocked. He must have been paralyzed with fear. He was not expecting to see his father yet. He didn't know what to think. Maybe his father was enraged that this "dead son" was daring to return. Maybe his father was running toward him in a rage.

And then, there was ... *that* moment. That moment. *The* moment. That life-changing moment when the son looked his father in the eye. That moment. *The* moment when the father looked into his son's eyes. When time stopped, and "his father saw him and had compassion." *Compassion* means to suffer *with* someone. Imagine the piercing moment when the son realized that his father was not enraged but instead was suffering. Imagine the intensity of the moment when the son realized that the father was not angry but instead was overcome with "deep tenderness" for his son who was suffering.

Imagine that moment. *The* moment. Be there in that moment.

For Your Prayer

Today, close your eyes and visualize all that is above, except put yourself in the place of the son. Jesus, this Jesus that you have come to know in a deeply personal way, is running toward you. Imagine yourself in that scene above. Invest the time needed today for your personal prayer.

What words stood out to you as you prayed?
What did you find stirring in your heart?

_____

_____

_____

_____

_____

_____

_____

_____

_____

_____

_____

_____

_____

_____

_____

_____

_____

_____

_____

_____

_____

_____

_____

_____

None

"But the father said to his servants, 'Bring quickly the best robe, and put it on him; and put a ring on his hand, and shoes on his feet; and bring the fatted calf and kill it, and let us eat and make merry; for this my son was dead, and is alive again; he was lost, and is found.' And they began to make merry."

—LUKE 15:22-24

None of what the son feared happened. *None.* In fact, in contrast to his fear of becoming a slave in his father's house, the son was actually adorned with "the best robe," "a ring on his hand," and "shoes on his feet" (Luke 15:22). Contrary to the anger and shame he feared, the son's arrival was met with a celebration, with "the fatted calf" and a call to "eat and make merry" (Luke 15:23).

None of what the son feared came to fruition. *None.*

I distinctly remember a moment in my life when I was struggling with a personal situation. The circumstances were not important, but my response to them was. I was ashamed of what I had done and angry at myself for my selfishness. The worst was at night. When the lights were out, all I could do was stare at the ceiling. That is when it would hit me the worst: the shame, guilt, and recrimination. It was then that my mind felt like a prison. My imagination would harass me, and my thoughts would only elicit more shame and fear.

One particular evening, it seemed worse than ever. My mind was racing. I could feel my thoughts claiming my identity. I felt ... just like the Prodigal Son. And then there was ... *that* moment. That moment. *The* moment. I remember with vivid clarity Jesus saying to me, "Who are you talking to? All the thoughts are in your head. Who are you talking to? You are not talking to me. You are talking to yourself. I am here, and I am ready for you to talk to me whenever you are ready."

What followed was a liberating moment with the Lord. As I poured out my heart to the person of Jesus Christ, I was relieved that none of what I was imagining was real. All the shame, all the guilt, all the fear, all that was *me* talking to *me*. The moment that I actually had the courage to face the Lord and speak to him felt like the moment when the Prodigal Son faced the father. None of what the son feared actually happened. *None.* And none of what I feared happened either. *None.*

Listen to me: None of what you fear will happen with God will come to fruition. *None.* The key is to stop ruminating and start relating. Do not be afraid. Jesus waits ... and there is nothing to be afraid of.

<hr>

For Your Prayer

Today, close your eyes and visualize all that is above, but put yourself in the son's place. Jesus, this Jesus whom you are coming to know in a deeply personal way, embraces you and welcomes you home. All that is above, imagine yourself in that scene. Invest the time needed today for your personal prayer.

What words stood out to you as you prayed?
What did you find stirring in your heart?

_____

_____

_____

_____

_____

_____

_____

_____

_____

_____

_____

_____

_____

_____

_____

_____

_____

_____

_____

_____

_____

_____

_____

_____

_____

_____

_____

_____

_____

Specific

"For this my son was dead, and is alive again;
he was lost, and is found."

—LUKE 15:24

I would like to return again to *Deus Caritas Est*. In the introduction, I mentioned that Pope Benedict XVI wrote, "We have come to believe in God's love: in these words the Christian can express the fundamental decision of his life. Being Christian is not the result of an ethical choice or a lofty idea, but the encounter with an event, a person, which gives life a new horizon and a decisive direction."[5]

In my experience as a priest, I have found that for most people, the "encounter with an event, a person, which gives life a new horizon and a decisive direction" is usually an encounter with God's mercy and forgiveness. This encounter is most life-changing when it is specific. We sin in very specific ways. We hurt others, ourselves, and the Lord himself in very specific ways. The more specific we are in our repentance, the more particular the gift of mercy.

Do you ever wonder what happened with the Prodigal Son? Do you wonder what happened once the feast was over? The Bible does not tell us the rest of the story, but, if I were a betting man, I would bet that what happened next was "I'm sorry." There was surely that moment when the Prodigal Son looked his father in the eye and apologized. And while the *father* may not have needed to hear it, the *son* needed to say it. The son needed to name his sins specifically so that he could receive the fullness of his father's forgiveness and love.

Likewise, we do not share with Jesus the specific details of our lives for his sake. We do so for ours. We disclose *every* detail of life with him because doing so, while we are vulnerable, fosters depth and intimacy.

As with the other Wednesdays this Lent, I would like you to return yet again to Matthew 16. Trust the process of repetition, and return to this passage, for it is the theme of this Lent. Be there again, and hear the questions anew in the light of this week's prayer.

What words stood out to you as you prayed?
What did you find stirring in your heart?

_____

_____

_____

_____

_____

_____

_____

_____

_____

_____

_____

_____

_____

_____

_____

_____

_____

_____

_____

_____

_____

_____

_____

_____

The Woman Caught in Adultery

Knew

"*Teacher, this woman has been caught in the act of adultery.*"

—JOHN 8:4

Thursday of the Fourth Week of Lent

Today, we shift our attention to the Gospel for the fifth Sunday of Lent: John 8:1-11, the story of the woman who was caught in adultery. The story of the Prodigal Son is the most popular of Jesus' parables. But, in my experience, this next Gospel passage has just as much of an impact, or, perhaps, even more, on those who take the time to really enter the scene. Maybe this is because so many people today struggle or have struggled with sexual sin. Maybe this story affects people because of the dramatic circumstances of the imminent stoning and Jesus' heroic confrontation with her accusers. Or, perhaps, the narrative strikes a chord within us because Jesus already knew her sin and still chose to protect her and fight for her.

Jesus already knew. In John 8:3-4, we read, "The scribes and the Pharisees brought a woman who had been caught in adultery, and placing her in the midst they said to him, 'Teacher, this woman has been caught in the act of adultery.'" The scribes and the Pharisees inform Jesus of her sin, but Jesus already knew. It is not as if Jesus was planning on helping her only to change his mind once he discovered what she had done. No, Jesus knew, and still he was resolved to help her.

Yesterday, I mentioned that we do not share with Jesus the specific details of our lives for his sake. We do so for ours. We disclose every detail of life with him because doing so, while vulnerable, fosters depth and intimacy. Jesus already knows the struggles, sufferings, and sins of your life. He already knows. And still he fights for *you*.

In fact, Jesus is the one who invited you into this Lent. Jesus is the one who placed the desire in your heart for this book. Jesus is the one who invited you to spend time with him, enter into imaginative prayer, and fall in love with him. Jesus did all this, and he did so fully aware of everything that you have ever done.

Jesus is never surprised. It is not as if Jesus wanted you to fall in love with him but then, as Lent began, he "discovered" things about you and then changed his mind. It is not as if he said to himself, "Well, if I had known that, I would never ..."

No. Jesus already knew you, and still he called you.

For Your Prayer

Today, read John 8:1-11. Read it slowly. Take your time. Once you have read the passage, close your eyes and enter the scene. You are the woman. You are standing in front of Jesus, only a few inches away from him, with your head bowed, terrified. You hear the shouts of your accusers behind you. You know they are gripping stones to hurl at you. You hear scratching as Jesus writes in the sand. Now, you hear his voice and feel the thump of stones on the ground as your accusers drop them and walk away. And then, when they leave ... you raise your head and look at Jesus. Take your time, be in the scene, and ask the Lord to guide you as you pray.

What words stood out to you as you prayed?
What did you find stirring in your heart?

Category

"The act of adultery."

—JOHN 8:4

Friday of the Fourth Week of Lent

Today, we continue to prepare for this coming Sunday, the fifth Sunday of Lent, by entering again into the Gospel story that will be read at Sunday's Mass: John 8:1-11.

Here is the scene. A woman has been caught in the act of adultery. The Mosaic Law is very clear. She was to be stoned to death in punishment for the sin. We can imagine that she was dragged through the village the way an animal is caught and dragged by hunters. They push her forward to stand in front of Jesus.

They stand behind her, the scribes and the Pharisees, each of them teeming with righteousness. They each bend down, looking around, hunting for the perfect rock to hurl so that they can crush her to death.

They do not see a woman. They do not see a person. They see a category. To them she is a category, a thing with a label: "an adulteress." They are ready to stone her, to kill her, because they want to remove the category.

Jesus does not see a category; he sees a woman. Jesus sees a person. Jesus sees this particular person. To Jesus she is not a category: "adulteress." No, she is a person. She is a person who has made an egregious mistake, but she is a person who can be forgiven.

Often, in the wake of our struggle, suffering, or sin, we ruminate and fall prey to self-recrimination and self-accusation. It is then that the whispers of the enemy attempt to claim our identity. During this assault, we are accused not of being someone who sinned but of being the sin itself. We become a category.

Common examples of recriminating categories include the following: "an adulterer" ... "a drunk" ... "a failure" ... "a mistake" ... "a fraud" ... "an addict" ... or fill in the blank.

The truth is this: You are not a category. You are a person, and the person of Jesus stands ready to fight for you.

For Your Prayer

Read John 8:1-11, as you did yesterday. Read it slowly. Take your time. Once you have read the passage, close your eyes, and enter the scene. You are the woman. You are standing in front of Jesus, only a few inches away from him, with your head bowed, terrified. You hear the shouts of your accusers behind you. You know they are gripping stones to hurl at you. You hear scratching as Jesus writes in the sand. Now you hear his voice and feel the thump of stones on the ground as your accusers drop them and walk away.

In the scene, you are just a thing, a category in their eyes. Listen to the way they accuse you. Listen to the specific way they label you. Now listen to Jesus' voice. Raise your head, and look at him. In Jesus' eyes, you are a person. Take your time, be in the scene, and ask the Lord to guide you as you pray.

What words stood out to you as you prayed?
What did you find stirring in your heart?

_____
_____
_____
_____
_____
_____
_____
_____
_____
_____
_____
_____
_____
_____
_____
_____
_____
_____
_____
_____
_____
_____
_____
_____
_____

Sees

"Jesus looked up and said to her, 'Woman.'"

—JOHN 8:10

Saturday of the Fourth Week of Lent

As we continue to prepare for tomorrow, Sunday of the Fifth Week of Lent, we will unpack more of the story of the woman who was caught in the act of adultery. As I prayed with John 8:1-11, I was moved by Jesus and his tenderness. As I placed myself in the scene, seeing what Jesus saw, hearing what he heard, and feeling what he felt, I was also moved to know that Jesus did not see a category; he saw a person. But I experienced a new insight as well: Jesus also saw the circumstances in her life that had led her to sin. Jesus knew what led her to sin and still loved her.

1 Samuel 16:7 states, "The LORD sees not as man sees; man looks on the outward appearance, but the LORD looks on the heart." God not only knows our sin, but he also knows how we got there. Far too often, when I look at my struggle, suffering, and sin, all I can see is the mistake, its consequences, and my failure. With this limited view, it is difficult for me to have compassion for myself or forgive myself.

That is the danger of ruminating instead of relating. Just a few days ago, on Tuesday, I shared how, on one particular evening, my ruminating was worse than ever, my mind was racing, and I could hear my thoughts claiming my identity. I shared with you how I remembered with vivid clarity Jesus say to me, "Who are you talking to? All the thoughts are in your head. Who are you talking to? You are not talking to me. You are talking to yourself. I am here, and I am ready for you to talk to me whenever you are ready."

When we ruminate about our sin, we never see the whole story. But when we are *with* Jesus in the moment, we can hear his reply to our struggle. He can reveal to us not only what we did but also why we did it, how we got there, and what we were searching for.

Much of our sin is medicinal—we use it to self-medicate. What I mean is that when I have a headache, I take aspirin. I take medicine so that I stop feeling the pain. The same is true with sin. Often sin is the "medicine" we grasp so that we can stop feeling pain.

Ask the Lord to reveal to you what you do not see about your life. Ask him to show you what he sees.

For Your Prayer

Read John 8:1-11, as you did yesterday. Read it slowly. Take your time. Once you have read the passage, close your eyes and enter the scene. You are the woman. You are standing in front of Jesus, only a few inches away from him, with your head bowed. You are terrified. Somehow, you understand that Jesus sees all the circumstances that got you where you are. He knows more about you than you do.

Take your time, be in the scene, and ask the Lord to reveal the particular circumstances that led to your own struggle, suffering, or sin. Ask the Lord to guide you as you pray.

What words stood out to you as you prayed?
What did you find stirring in your heart?

Mercy

*"Woman, where are they? Has
no one condemned you?"*

—JOHN 8:10

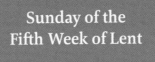

The heart of today's Gospel on this fifth Sunday of Lent is this:

> Jesus bent down and wrote with his finger on the ground.
> And as they continued to ask him, he stood up and said to
> them, "Let him who is without sin among you be the first
> to throw a stone at her." And once more he bent down and
> wrote with his finger on the ground. But when they heard
> it, they went away, one by one, beginning with the eldest,
> and Jesus was left alone with the woman standing before
> him. Jesus looked up and said to her, "Woman, where are
> they? Has no one condemned you?" (John 8:6b-10)

Instead of a gruesome stoning and death, the woman is saved. She
is forgiven. She receives mercy. In my *Lenten Companion* for the
liturgical year A, I offered commentary on Jesus' interaction with
the Samaritan woman at the well and mentioned that someone
once said, "They only call it mercy when you don't deserve it." That
applies again today. Jesus shows mercy to the woman in today's
Gospel, and they only call it mercy when you don't deserve it.

The woman caught in adultery does not deserve Jesus' mercy.
Actually, according to Mosaic Law, she deserves to be stoned.
Jesus, however, gives her far more than she deserves. She does
not deserve to be saved, but she is saved anyway.

I struggle with forgiveness as perhaps you do too. I struggle to
forgive others. I struggle to forgive myself. I struggle to receive the
fullness of God's forgiveness. Why? Because I hold in my heart a
false judgment—the idea that you have to be worthy of forgiveness,
you have to deserve to be forgiven. That is why so many of us
will not forgive those who hurt us or will not forgive ourselves.
We do not feel they deserve it. We do not feel we deserve it. That
is also why many of us wait so long to allow the Lord to forgive
us. We keep trying to *earn* his forgiveness in a variety of ways.

Listen to me: You do not deserve his love. You never have, and you never will. You do not deserve his forgiveness. You never have, and you never will. You do not deserve his mercy. You never have. You never will.

The good news is ... he gives it all to you anyway.

For Your Prayer

Again, like yesterday, read John 8:1-11. Read it slowly. Take your time. Once you have read the passage, close your eyes and enter the scene. You are the woman. You are standing in front of Jesus, only a few inches away from him, with your head bowed. You are terrified. Soon you realize that everyone is gone. You know you do not deserve to be forgiven.

Take your time, be in the scene, and ask the Lord to reveal the depths of his mercy. Ask the Lord to guide you as you pray.

What words stood out to you as you prayed?
What did you find stirring in your heart?

_____
_____
_____
_____
_____
_____
_____
_____
_____
_____
_____
_____
_____
_____
_____
_____
_____
_____
_____
_____
_____
_____
_____
_____
_____
_____

*"Jesus was left alone with the woman
standing before him."*

—JOHN 8:9

Today's meditation is the thirty-fourth meditation in this book. I do not assume that you remember everything, but a few things are so important that they periodically resurface and require our attention. Therefore, I would like to take you back to what I said on the third Sunday of Lent, where I shared one of my favorite passages from Pope Benedict XVI's *Deus Caritas Est*:

> Love of neighbour is thus shown to be possible in the way proclaimed by the Bible, by Jesus. It consists in the very fact that, in God and with God, I love even the person whom I do not like or even know. This can only take place on the basis of an intimate encounter with God, an encounter which has become a communion of will, even affecting my feelings. Then I learn to look on this other person not simply with my eyes and my feelings, but from the perspective of Jesus Christ. ... Seeing with the eyes of Christ, I can give to others much more than their outward necessities; I can give them the look of love which they crave.[6]

This quote carries with it *the* theme of this book and *the* grace that disposes us to fall in love. In fact, if you have not done so already, stop reading for a moment, and take time to digest that quote.

There is an essential connection between being loved and being seen. This is true for all of humanity, and it was true for the woman caught in adultery. As I prayed with John 8:1-11, I was struck by the moment when all her accusers have left. Jesus has exposed the scribes and the Pharisees as he writes in the sand. Her accusers have dropped their stones and fled. Then, in a quiet moment that stops time itself, "Jesus was left alone with the woman standing before him" (John 8:9).

She is alone. She is alone with Jesus. And now she has to decide whether to look at him. As I prayed with this Gospel story, this was the moment when I felt her vulnerability. It is strange to say that most of us would feel more vulnerable facing Jesus than facing our accusers. To be seen in the pure and personal way that Jesus sees a person can be a vulnerable experience. The woman would have had to choose to face Jesus. She would have had to choose to be seen by him.

For Your Prayer

Again, read John 8:1-11. Read it slowly. Take your time. Once you have read the passage, close your eyes, and enter the scene. You are the woman. You are standing in front of Jesus, only a few inches away from him, with your head bowed. You are terrified. Soon you realize that everyone is gone. You know you do not deserve to be forgiven. And now, you have to choose to look up and let yourself look Jesus in the eye.

Take your time, be in the scene, and ask the Lord to reveal the depths of his mercy.
Ask the Lord to guide you as you pray.

What words stood out to you as you prayed?
What did you find stirring in your heart?

Never

"Neither do I condemn you."

—JOHN 8:11

When I was in the seminary, I was lucky enough to have the best spiritual director in the house. Fr. H. was a passionate lover of Jesus who lived the kind of priesthood that I strove and still strive for. It was a time in my life when I was struggling with a particular sin. I could not turn the corner, and I became discouraged. Soon, I disclosed my heart in spiritual direction. In that moment, as he was Jesus to me, Fr. H. was both gentle and wise. I will never forget what he said: "Both the devil and the Lord can say the same thing. It's not the words but the way it affects you that will reveal who's speaking." This is what he meant:

At that point in seminary, I was only a year away from ordination. I was beginning to feel an urgency, as if there was not enough time. I was beginning to fear my personal struggles with virtue and kept hearing the words "You cannot do this. You will always need help." Fr. H. helped me see how both the devil and the Lord might be using the same words but were not saying the same thing.

In moments of temptation and struggle, the enemy would whisper, "You cannot do this. You will always need help." Those words made me feel unworthy. I felt accused. I felt condemned. I thought, "I cannot do this. I will never be able to do this." Notice that when the enemy spoke these words, I focused on what I could not do.

In contrast, in moments of prayer Jesus would say gently, "You cannot do this. You will always need help." These same words, because of who said them, felt different. I thought, "That's right. I can't do this. But then again, who can? I'll always need help, so Jesus please help me." Notice that when Jesus spoke the same words, they made me aware of what he could do in me.

When the Prodigal Son had the courage to look at his father, none of his fears came true. Likewise, when the woman caught in adultery had the courage to look at Jesus, none of her fears came true. Jesus said to her, "'Woman, where are they? Has no one condemned you?' She said, 'No one, Lord.' And Jesus said, 'Neither do I condemn you; go, and do not sin again'" (John 8:10-11).

Jesus did not condemn her. Jesus never condemns. Both the devil and the Lord can speak to us about our sin, but because of who is speaking, the way we hear it will be very different.

For Your Prayer

Again, read John 8:1-11. Read it slowly. Take your time. Once you have read the passage, close your eyes, and enter the scene. You are the woman. You choose to look up and look Jesus in the eye. Hear the words he spoke to her as they are spoken to you. Take your time, be in the scene, and ask the Lord to reveal the depths of his mercy. Ask the Lord to guide you as you pray.

What words stood out to you as you prayed?
What did you find stirring in your heart?

_____
_____
_____
_____
_____
_____
_____
_____
_____
_____
_____
_____
_____
_____
_____
_____
_____
_____
_____
_____
_____
_____
_____
_____

More

"But who do you say that I am?"

—MATTHEW 16:15

Who is he? Who is this Jesus that you are falling in love with? Jesus is a real man. He experienced vulnerability. He had needs. He was dependent. He experienced temptation. As you have come to experience his humanity, he has become more approachable, easier to be with, and safer to relate to. However, Jesus is not merely a human; he is also fully divine. We have shed the façade of who he is not. He is not merely a historical figure or merely *a* teacher or merely *a* way to get to heaven. He is God, and he has the power to change your life.

Jesus, this Jesus you are falling in love with, does not see you the way you see you. Jesus sees you through the lens of love because Jesus is love. Love is not something Jesus does—love is who Jesus is. He is pure love, and, as such, Jesus sees us without our familiar lens and judgments, which cloak us with a false identity. Jesus sees us as we are, as we always have been in his eyes.

Jesus, this Jesus you are falling in love with, is like the father in the story of the Prodigal Son. He is the one waiting for you. His heart is filled with anticipation and compassion for you. No matter how worthy you feel of his love, he brims with anticipation of giving himself to you. He is also passionately concerned about your soul and your eternal salvation. He loves you with a deep tenderness, especially when you are suffering.

Jesus, this Jesus you are falling in love with, is the same Jesus who showed mercy to the woman caught in adultery. You are not a category. You are a person, and he stands ready to fight for you. He already knows the struggles, sufferings, and sins of your life.

You do not deserve his mercy. You never have, and you never will. But they only call it mercy when you do not deserve it.

Who is he? Who is this Jesus that you are falling in love with? I would like you to return yet again to Matthew 16, as you have on the previous Wednesdays of Lent. Once again, trust the process of repetition, of returning to this passage each week, for it is the theme of this Lent. Be there again, and hear the questions anew.

For Your Prayer

Once again today, read Matthew 16:13-15. Imagine that you and Jesus and the apostles have been sitting around a campfire. Return to the scene. Imagine you are there with Jesus. The apostles have gone to bed, and it is just you and Jesus alone. You are next to him. With great love in his eyes, Jesus looks deep into your eyes. He begins to tell you the story of the woman caught in adultery. He tells you the story from his perspective. As you listen, you recall the particular moments in your life when you could have been in her place.

After moments when he shares much more with you and you share your heart with him, imagine that Jesus looks at you and asks, "Who do you say that I am?" Answer the question from your heart. Then, have the courage to ask, "Who do you say that I am, Lord?" Let him respond. Ask him to reveal how he sees you.

What words stood out to you as you prayed?
What did you find stirring in your heart?

_____
_____
_____
_____
_____
_____
_____
_____
_____
_____
_____
_____
_____
_____
_____
_____
_____
_____
_____
_____
_____
_____
_____
_____
_____

Gethsemane

Love

"Do you love me?"

—JOHN 21:15

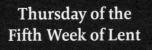

Today, we shift our attention to the Gospel that awaits us this coming Sunday. However, next week is not just any week; it is Holy Week. As I did in last year's *Lenten Companion*, I would like to offer a few insights to help us appreciate the reality of Holy Week.

In Hebrew, the word for *holy* comes from the same root as *sacred* or *consecrated*. *To consecrate* means "to set apart." Things that are sacred, things that are holy, are consecrated; they are set apart. Thus, Holy Week next week is sacred; it is set apart from every other week, and it will look, feel, and be different. It is holy, it is consecrated, and it is set apart precisely because of the events we celebrate during it—namely, the suffering, death, and resurrection of Jesus.

If next week is going to be different, we need to rethink the way we approach Holy Week. How can we set apart this time to enter into the reality of Jesus' suffering, death, and resurrection?

Next week must be different. This Lent has been different. You are different. The way you see Jesus is different. So much has happened between you and Jesus.

In the introduction to this book, I shared with you a quote from Fr. Joseph Whelan:

> Nothing is more practical than finding God, than falling in Love in a quite absolute, final way. What you are in love with, what seizes your imagination, will affect everything. It will decide what will get you out of bed in the morning, what you do with your evenings, how you spend your weekends, what you read, whom you know, what breaks your heart, and what amazes you with joy and gratitude. Fall in Love, stay in love, and it will decide everything.[7]

Holy Week is about love. The Last Supper, the Cross, and the Resurrection are all about love.

The best way to prepare for the week is to be with Jesus. And, today, he has a different question for you.

For Your Prayer

Today, read John 21:15. This is a post-Resurrection account, but, for a moment, please disregard that. Trust the process, and imagine that you are there with Jesus. It is just the two of you. He, this Jesus you have been with, looks deep into your eyes with great love. He looks at you and asks you, "Do you love me?" Answer the question from your heart. Answer the question in whatever way is natural.

Then, have the courage to ask him the same question: "Lord, do you love me?" Let him respond. Ask him to reveal how he feels for you.

What words stood out to you as you prayed?
What did you find stirring in your heart?

Intentional

"Do you love me?"

—JOHN 21:16

As I did in last year's *Lenten Companion,* I would like to offer a few practical encouragements to help you appreciate the reality of Holy Week. Let me reiterate that if next week is going to be consecrated, we must prepare for it well and be ready to receive everything God wants to offer us. In the Old Testament, God taught his Chosen People how to prepare for worship. It is important for us, too, to prepare with care for Holy Week so that we may observe these holy days as they are meant to be observed.

In last year's *Lenten Companion,* I mentioned that there are three things we must include in our preparation. First, we must be intentional. The celebration of Holy Week will not just happen. Unless we carve out time, we will not be able to prepare or observe the holy days well. Second, we must be prepared to make sacrifices. Most of us are overextended with our busy schedules. If we are going to have more time, we will have to be honest about the need to let go of some things. We may have to change our rhythm at night to celebrate Holy Thursday. This may mean taking a day off from work on Good Friday. Third, we need to pay attention to the details. For example, what time are services at your parish? Now is the time to find out, to begin thinking about next week. Now is the time to prepare.

May I also invite you to begin to reread your journal. Return to the moments when Jesus was closest. Revisit the passages that most disposed you to intimacy. So much has *already* happened. Let yourself breathe a little as you prepare for the intensity of next week.

Once again, trust the process of repetition, returning to *the* question of your heart. Be there again, and hear the question anew.

For Your Prayer

Today, read John 21:16. As before, disregard the fact that this is a post-Resurrection account. Trust the process, and imagine you are there with Jesus. It is just the two of you. He, this Jesus you have been with, looks deep into your eyes with great love. He looks at you and asks you, "Do you love me?" Answer the question from your heart. Answer the question in whatever way is natural.

Then, have the courage to ask him the same question: "Lord, do you love me?" Let him respond. Ask him to reveal how he feels for you.

Ways to Prepare

- Call your local parish or visit its website. Find out the dates, times, and locations of Holy Week services.

- Think through Holy Thursday night: What will it take for you to make it? What is the best way for your family to pray through the day together?

- Think through Good Friday: Can you take off from work or school? Is it possible to set the day aside as a full day of prayer? What is the best way for your family to pray through the day together?

- Think through Holy Saturday: It is not Easter yet. Jesus remains in the tomb. How can you keep a quiet and prayerful spirit in your home on this day?

- Think through Easter Sunday: What will it take for you and your family to be able to pray in the midst of other plans you may have?

What words stood out to you as you prayed?
What did you find stirring in your heart?

Unplug

"Do you love me?"

—JOHN 21:17

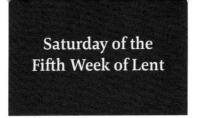

In last year's *Lenten Companion,* I challenged readers on the Saturday before Holy Week, as I will again today.

To prepare for Holy Week, I would like to present again three distinct ways we can get ready. First, we can fast from using our smartphones. If we have the courage to be honest, most of us do not use our smartphones mainly as phones. We use them as entertainment or information devices—in other words, as distractions. To be clear: I am not recommending that we completely ignore our smartphones or even turn them off. I am recommending that we use them only as phones—as communications devices—and to fast from using them to surf the internet, listen to music, engage in social media, or purchase things. Apart from essential emails, text messages, or calls, can you fast from using your smartphone this week? Do you have the discipline to fast from these forms of distraction?

Second, we can fast from other exterior "noise"—this means no radio, television, or music. Intentionally creating exterior silence can have a dramatic impact on our availability to experience interior silence. We quickly discover how distracting the constant noise in our lives is. We also discover the quiet, subtle voice of God, who has always been speaking to us but has often been drowned out in all the noise. Do you have the discipline and self-possession necessary to intentionally create more silence in your life?

Third, we can fast in the traditional way—from food and alcohol. Fasting from alcohol means giving it up entirely. Fasting from food means no snacks between meals; it also means limiting the amount of food you eat in three meals to the equivalent of just two regular meals. Eating less and avoiding alcohol creates a hunger within us, and physical hunger is meant to elicit spiritual hunger. Creating more space in our bodies has a direct influence on creating more space in our hearts.

These might sound like extreme suggestions. Most of us would struggle with one of these, so you might ask if you can really do all three. You can! You deserve to challenge yourself, and God deserves your full effort next week. Because next week is not like any other week; it is *the* week. Fasting from our smartphones, noise, and food is a small sacrifice in comparison to how much God is offering us.

For Your Prayer

Today, read John 21:17. As before, disregard the fact that this is a post-Resurrection account. Trust the process, and imagine you are there with Jesus. It is just the two of you. He, this Jesus you have been with, looks deep into your eyes with great love. He looks at you and asks, "Do you love me?" Answer the question from your heart. Answer the question in whatever way is natural.

Then, have the courage to ask him the same question: "Lord, do you love me?" Let him respond. Ask him to reveal how he feels for you.

What words stood out to you as you prayed?
What did you find stirring in your heart?

Introduction to
HOLY WEEK

*"[Christ] became obedient unto death,
even death on a cross."*
—PHILIPPIANS 2:8

Holy Week is unlike any other week. The next eight days are consecrated and set apart for God. This week's meditations are different from the previous weeks as well. They shift from meditations based on the Sunday Gospel readings to scenes from Holy Week with Jesus and those closest to him. These guided imaginative prayers are designed to help you open your heart more fully to him through the events of his passion and death.

In the introduction to his book *Meditation and Contemplation,* Fr. Timothy Gallagher, OMV, describes Ignatian contemplation as a way of praying in which we see the people in a Scripture passage, hear their words as they speak, and observe their actions.[8] This imaginative engagement with Scripture is a time-tested way of drawing closer to the Lord. While this week's scenes are drawn directly from Scripture, imagined details have been added to help us more personally experience Jesus, with whom we have fallen in love this Lent and who acts in your life and in mine even today.

This week, I invite you to personally enter each guided meditation. Be *in* the scene. Be *with* Jesus.

See

*"The whole multitude of the disciples
began to rejoice and praise God."*

—LUKE 19:37

Palm Sunday

Welcome to Holy Week. Yes, it is indeed holy. Mass today will feel different. This week is set apart, and the difference in Mass today helps us to *feel* the difference. Before Mass, you will hear Luke's account of Jesus' entrance into Jerusalem on Palm Sunday. There, we read the following account:

> And throwing their garments on the colt they set Jesus upon it. And as he rode along, they spread their garments on the road. As he was now drawing near, at the descent of the Mount of Olives, the whole multitude of the disciples began to rejoice and praise God with a loud voice for all the mighty works that they had seen, saying, "Blessed is the King who comes in the name of the Lord! Peace in heaven and glory in the highest!" (Luke 19:35-38)

Notice that Luke says that "the whole multitude of the disciples began to rejoice and praise God with a loud voice." The *whole multitude*. That is a lot of people.

Enter into the scene with me now. Let us ask the Holy Spirit to guide your imagination so that you might see what they saw, hear what they heard, and feel what they felt.

Jesus sits atop the donkey. The apostles circle the donkey to protect the Lord from the crowd as *so many* people swarm around Jesus. The frenetic energy in the air is fueled by their hopes that Jesus will soon declare himself as the earthly king of the Jews and violently free them from their Roman oppressors. You are there. You are in the scene. You are walking on Jesus' right side as he sits on the donkey. You are so close to Jesus that your skin is pressed up against the coarse hair of the donkey. Occasionally, you can feel Jesus' leg sway and rub against your shoulder. You are there, right there with him.

There is a mob of people. So many have been waiting for Jesus in Jerusalem, *a whole multitude*. But from the midst of them, you can't really see how many there are. There are so many people pressing in on Jesus that it feels like at any moment, they might stampede. All you see is the mass of people. You can't see where you are going. You can't see what is happening, except for the excitement of the people immediately around you. People are frantically trying to touch Jesus. There is both excitement and panic in you because you can't see anything except the frenzy.

Then, suddenly, you feel *him*. You feel *his* hand. Jesus is leaning over on the donkey, and with his right hand he squeezes your left shoulder. Immediately you look up, and you see *him*. You see those eyes, the eyes you have looked into throughout this Lent. You are overcome with love and trust.

Looking deep into your eyes, Jesus says to you, "I see you. And I know you can't see anything but the mob. But I can see everything from up here. Trust me. Let me lead. Do not take your eyes off of me."

For Your Prayer

Be there with Jesus, and feel his eyes on you. Write about what it is like to be with Jesus on Palm Sunday. Pray through the feelings that arise as you linger in that moment.

What words stood out to you as you prayed?
What did you find stirring in your heart?

_____

_____

_____

_____

_____

_____

_____

_____

_____

_____

_____

_____

_____

_____

_____

_____

_____

_____

_____

_____

_____

_____

_____

_____

_____

Price

"*So from that day on they took counsel about how to put him to death.*"

—JOHN 11:53

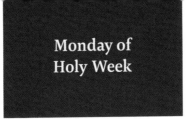

Enter into the scene with me now. Ask the Holy Spirit to guide your imagination so that you may see what they saw, hear what they heard, and feel what they felt.

The apostles have gone ahead to the Temple. Jesus asked you and the Blessed Mother to stay back with him for a few extra moments of prayer before the day begins. The three of you are now walking toward Jerusalem, as Jesus plans to teach in the Temple. Jesus is walking in the center with his mother on his left and you on his right.

You have spent so much time with Jesus. You have come to know the bounty of his joy, the well-spring of his compassion, and the tireless consistency of his patience, tenderness, and mercy. But, today, there is something different. He is different. He is focused, but not so much on the task at hand, the walking or the teaching he will do. No, he is focused ... on his Father. As you walk beside him, you can feel his communion with the Father radiating from him.

Mary is there beside him. You have come to love her also. You have come to notice that Jesus is a little different when she is with him. There is a way that he loves her that is beyond words. Her person brings peace, quiet, and stillness to the situation. But, today, she too is different. She seems wrapped in silence and prayer.

Let us imagine now an event the Gospels do not describe. Though this specific event may not have happened, Jesus' followers were surely aware of the increasing danger that Jesus was in.

As you walk with Jesus and Mary, your eyes are suddenly drawn up the hill to the figure of Peter sprinting frantically toward the three of you. Peter, a rock of brash passion, a "man's man," is different too. His eyes are streaming with tears. As he nears you, Jesus stops. Mary stops. You stop. And Peter tries to stop, but his momentum causes him to stumble into Jesus' arms. For a moment, there is silence. Then, Peter straightens and says, "There is a price on your head. They took counsel on how to put you to death."

Peter's words are like shards of ice in your veins. You *love* Jesus. You love *him*. This Jesus whom you love—there is now a price on his head, and the authorities are seeking to kill him. Your eyes fill with tears; your heart drops. Your mind races, grasping at what this means. Your imagination races to the worst as you think, "Surely, not death. Surely ... not ... crucifixion."

Then, like yesterday, you feel *his* hand. With his right hand he squeezes your left shoulder. You see those eyes, the eyes you have looked into throughout this Lent. You are overcome with love and trust.

Looking deep into your eyes, Jesus says, "Look at me. Trust me. Let me lead. Do not take your eyes off of me."

For Your Prayer

Be there with Jesus, and feel his eyes on you. Write about what it is like to be with Jesus now. Pray through the feelings that arise as you linger in this moment.

What words stood out to you as you prayed?
What did you find stirring in your heart?

Mom

"And a sword will pierce through your own soul also."

—LUKE 2:35

It is late at night, and you find yourself in a familiar but sacred space—by a campfire. The fire is fading, growing smaller as the night deepens, draping the scene like a warm blanket. Everyone has fallen asleep except you, Jesus, and his *mom*. The three of you sit close: Jesus in the middle, his mom on his left, and you on his right.

Enter into the scene with me now. Let us ask the Holy Spirit to guide your imagination so that you might see what they saw, hear what they heard, and feel what they felt.

The intensity of these past few days has changed the mood. Somewhat intentionally, Jesus redirects conversation in order to share a bit of joy. With a smile too deep for words, he looks at his mom and says, "Tell us the story." *The* story.

Mary's face lights up with delight. She leans across Jesus and grabs your hand. As she does this, Jesus feels squeezed in the middle of the two of you and laughs, for he loves it when people hear *the story*.

Mary begins. She tells in great detail about the house where she lived with her parents when she and Joseph were betrothed. She tells you about the Annunciation. She tells you about Joseph, how they met, and the man he was. The memory of Joseph brings a joyful tear to her eyes. Mary releases your hand, takes Jesus' hand, and the two of them remember Joseph with a sacred affection.

Mary tells you the story of the census, the pilgrimage to Bethlehem, and the birth. She tells you about the visit of the shepherds and about Jesus' presentation in the Temple. Then, suddenly, her cadence slows. Her voice softens. More solemn now, she tells the story of Simeon. She looks into Jesus' eyes as if she is looking into her past as she recounts the words Simeon spoke to her: "Behold, this child is set for the fall and rising of many in Israel, and for a sign that is spoken against (and a sword will pierce through your own soul also), that thoughts out of many hearts may be revealed" (Luke 2:34-35).

You listen hungrily to every word, but the words about a sword piercing Mary's heart pierce your heart now too. You are moved. Staring at Jesus' mom, your eyes fill with tears. You are suspended in the moment. You don't want her to be hurt. You want to protect her.

Then, suddenly again, you feel *him*. You feel *his* hand. With his right hand he squeezes your left shoulder. You see those eyes, the eyes you have looked into throughout this Lent. You are overcome with love and trust.

Looking deep into your eyes, Jesus says to you, "Look at me. Trust me. Do not be afraid. Do not take your eyes off of me."

For Your Prayer

Be there with Jesus, and feel his eyes on you. Write about what it is like to be with Jesus. Pray through the feelings that arise as you linger in this moment.

What words stood out to you as you prayed?
What did you find stirring in your heart?

_____

_____

_____

_____

_____

_____

_____

_____

_____

_____

_____

_____

_____

_____

_____

_____

_____

_____

_____

_____

_____

_____

_____

_____

Campfire

"Abide in me."

—JOHN 15:4

You may never sit by a campfire in the same way. Over the past forty-three days, I have invited you to pray in the scene of the campfire fifteen times. This was intentional. The repetition is meant to sear the image of the campfire into your imagination so that it will become a place you can return to with Jesus for the rest of your life.

Let us go back to where we began with the quotation from *Deus Caritas Est* by Pope Benedict XVI: "Being Christian is not the result of an ethical choice or a lofty idea, but the encounter with an event, a person, which gives life a new horizon and a decisive direction."[9] This is what the campfire has become: a place of encounter. Here at the campfire, you have encountered him in such a way that he has given you "a new horizon and a decisive direction."

You cannot go back to life as it was before Ash Wednesday. Too much has changed. He is different. You are different.

So, I ask you one final time, who is he? Who is this Jesus whom you have fallen in love with? As on the previous Wednesdays, I would like you to return again to Matthew 16. Once again, trust the process of repetition, returning to this passage that expresses the theme of this Lent. Be there again, and hear the questions anew.

For Your Prayer

*Once again today, return to the campfire. Imagine
you are there with Jesus. It is just the two of you. You
are right next to him. Jesus looks deep into your eyes
with great love. He begins to tell you everything that
is going to happen over the next few days. His words
shock you. Betrayal. Arrest. Torture. Crucifixion.
And then he says that other word: death.*

*After moments when he shares much more with you,
and you share your heart with him, imagine that Jesus
looks at you and asks, "Who do you say that I am?"
Answer the question from your heart. Then, have the
courage to ask, "Who do you say that I am, Lord?" Let
him respond. Ask him to reveal how he sees you.*

*Soon, he looks at you and asks, "Do you love me?"
Answer the question from your heart. Answer
the question in whatever way is natural.*

*Then, have the courage to ask him the same
question: "Do you love me?" Let him respond.
Ask him to reveal how he feels for you.*

*Now imagine that you feel him. You feel his hand.
With his right hand he squeezes your left hand. You see
those eyes, the eyes you have looked into throughout
this Lent. You are overcome with love and trust.*

*Looking deep into your eyes, Jesus says, "Look at
me. Trust me. Do not be afraid. These next few
days will be beyond what you imagine. Listen
to me: Do not take your eyes off of me."*

What words stood out to you as you prayed?
What did you find stirring in your heart?

_____

_____

_____

_____

_____

_____

_____

_____

_____

_____

_____

_____

_____

_____

_____

_____

_____

_____

_____

_____

_____

_____

_____

The Passion and Resurrection

Wash

"He poured water into a basin, and began to wash the disciples' feet, and to wipe them with the towel that was tied around him."

—JOHN 13:5

Holy Thursday

You are in the Upper Room. The sun has just set. It is time to celebrate the sacred Passover meal, commemorating the most important event in Jewish history. The preparations are complete. The apostles are gathered. You are there. You belong there.

Enter into the scene with me now. Let us ask the Holy Spirit to guide your imagination so that you may see what they saw, hear what they heard, and feel what they felt.

> Jesus, knowing that the Father had given all things into his hands, and that he had come from God and was going to God, rose from supper, laid aside his garments, and tied a towel around himself. Then he poured water into a basin, and began to wash the disciples' feet, and to wipe them with the towel that was tied around him. (John 13:3-5)

Jesus washes their feet one by one. As the evening began, he asked you personally to sit at his right. But now he moves from his left in a clockwise circle washing the feet of each apostle. This means you will be last, for he wanted to conclude with *your* feet.

As he washes the feet of the others, you notice every move. You notice the care with which he washes their feet. You notice the profound humility as he gently dries each foot. But you are most moved by his presence. With each of the apostles, Jesus is completely present in the moment. Jesus knows these men. He knows them better than they know themselves.

Now it is time … it is your turn. Jesus kneels before you. As with each of the others, he pauses in an extended silence, praying before he places his hands on your feet. He pours the water over each foot slowly, and, with his confident hands, he dries them with a soft linen towel. You are deeply moved with emotion and with memory. You remember the devil, the temptations, and the desert. You remember the Prodigal Son and the woman caught in adultery. You remember the campfire, the many campfires.

Then, you feel *him*. You feel *his* hands. His hands squeeze your hands to bring you back into the present moment. You see those eyes, the eyes you have looked into throughout this Lent. You are overcome with love and trust.

Looking deep into your eyes, Jesus says to you, "Look at me. Trust me. Do not be afraid. Listen to me: Do not be afraid. Do not take your eyes off of me."

For Your Prayer

Be there with Jesus, and feel his eyes on you. Write about what it is like to be with Jesus. Pray through the feelings that arise as you linger in this moment.

What words stood out to you as you prayed?
What did you find stirring in your heart?

Eyes

"Standing by the cross of Jesus were his mother, and his mother's sister, Mary the wife of Clopas, and Mary Magdalene."

—JOHN 19:25

Good Friday

E nter into the scene with me now. Let us ask the Holy Spirit to guide your imagination so that you might see what they saw, hear what they heard, and feel what they felt.

You are *there* ... at the Cross. All of Lent has led to this moment. You are kneeling at the base of the Cross. Your forehead is pressed into the wood of the Cross. You can feel splinters leaving marks on your skin. Your eyes are closed in homage. You can feel the sand and rock under your knees as you kneel.

Then, you feel something wet and cold drop onto your head. It slides slowly down, clinging to your cheek. You move your hand to your cheek to wipe it off, and you catch your breath when you realize it is blood. *His* blood.

You look up. Still kneeling, you lean back so that you can look up. At first, you see only his feet, which are mere inches from your eyes. Then, you see his knees, his waist, his ribs, and, finally, his eyes.

You see those eyes, the eyes you have looked into throughout this Lent. You are overcome with love. You are overcome with memory.

As you look into his eyes, you remember all that he has said to you this Lent. How many times did he ask you, "Who do you say that I am?" How many times did you ask, "Who do you say that *I* am, Lord?" How many times did he ask, "Do you love me?" How many times did you ask him the same?

Those eyes. His eyes. As you look into those eyes, you recall, "Nothing is more practical than finding God, than falling in Love in a quite absolute, final way. What you are in love with, what seizes your imagination, will affect everything. It will decide what will get you out of bed in the morning, what you do with your evenings, how you spend your weekends, what you read, whom you know, what breaks your heart, and what amazes you with joy and gratitude. Fall in Love, stay in love, and it will decide everything."[10]

As you stare into his eyes, take a moment to become aware of what is in your heart. How do you feel? What do you feel?

Now, in the midst of his agony, Jesus says to you, "Look at me. Trust me. Do not be afraid. Listen to me: Do *not* be afraid. You will see me again."

For Your Prayer

Be there with Jesus, and feel his eyes on you. Write about what it is like to be with Jesus. Pray through the feelings that arise as you linger in that moment.

What words stood out to you as you prayed?
What did you find stirring in your heart?

_____

_____

_____

_____

_____

_____

_____

_____

_____

_____

_____

_____

_____

_____

_____

_____

_____

_____

_____

_____

_____

_____

_____

_____

_____

Wait

"Standing by the cross of Jesus were ..."

—JOHN 19:25

Holy Saturday

It is Holy Saturday. Yesterday was an intense day, the most emotional day of your life. You were there for it all. You saw it all. The trials. The scourging. The crown of thorns. You saw him fall. You saw him nailed to the Cross. You saw him die on the Cross.

Enter into the scene with me now. Let us ask the Holy Spirit to guide your imagination.

You felt Jesus' blood run down your cheek as you looked him in the eye. You saw him take his last breath. You held his mother in your arms as she held him in hers. With others, you lifted his body into the tomb. You kissed his body as you said goodbye.

Then, you walked. You walked alone. *Alone.* You are *alone.*

He is gone. He is dead. It hurts to see those words. It hurts. You hurt.

You do the only thing you can—you return to a place that feels safe. You return ... to ... the ... campfire.

Wednesday, just a few days ago, was the last time you and he were together, alone, and it was around a campfire. The campfire feels like the safest place in the world, and so you return. You are there, in the same spot, sitting now where you sat then. You are there, the fire is there, but he is not. He is missing. You are *alone.*

He said he would die, but he said he would rise. You trust him. You know his words. You want to believe, but it is natural, in the flood of emotions, to doubt. Will he rise? Will you ever see him again?

You feel so ... *alone.* You miss him. You long for him. You cannot bear to think about life without him. You begin to weep. You begin to sob uncontrollably, for the one you love is gone.

All you can do is wait. All you can do is hope.

All you can do is remember. So you close your eyes, and it is as if you are back at the Cross again. You remember it as if it was happening all over again. He was looking deep into your eyes, and he said to you, "Look at me. Trust me. Do not be afraid. Listen to me: Do *not* be afraid. You will see me again."

For Your Prayer

Be there at the campfire, and remember his eyes on you. Write about what it is like to wait for Jesus. Pray through the feelings that arise as you linger in that moment.

What words stood out to you as you prayed?
What did you find stirring in your heart?

_____
_____
_____
_____
_____
_____
_____
_____
_____
_____
_____
_____
_____
_____
_____
_____
_____
_____
_____
_____
_____
_____
_____
_____
_____

Love

"Lord, you know everything; you know that I love you."

—JOHN 21:17

Last night was Holy Saturday. You fell asleep at the campfire. Exhausted, spent, and almost numb, you do not remember how or when you fell asleep, but you did.

Enter into the scene with me now. Let us ask the Holy Spirit to guide your imagination.

It is now early morning, and you are awakened by the splendor of the sky. The sunrise is glorious. This particular sunrise is extraordinary. It is as if the Father himself is showing off his power and glory.

You are captivated by the sunrise. You miss him. As you feel the pain in your heart, you watch the sunrise and, unthinkingly, whisper the words to yourself: "The sunrise. The sunrise. Sunrise." It is almost as if you are not speaking the words, but they are speaking to you. You continue to whisper, not knowing why or even how: "Sunrise. Sun ... rise. Sun. Rise." You remember him, the One you love, and you close your eyes in grief. Filled with emotion, you mutter the quietest whisper, "Rise." Again, in tears, you whisper, "Rise."

Racked with loneliness, racked with grief, you whisper "Rise." You whisper aloud, "He said he would rise." Again, you mutter in the quietest whisper, "Rise."

As you open your mouth one last time, you hear the word "Rise" spoken again, but not by you. Something is different. Another voice harmonizes with yours. Two voices say quietly, "Rise."

Your eyes are closed, and you are paralyzed with surprise. You sit there still, unable to move or open your eyes. The moment feels like forever. Then, you hear the other voice again, the one that is not your own. It is his voice, and he says, "Rise ... rise ... rise. I told you ... that ... I ... would ... rise."

Then, after the longest pause ever, he says to you, "Look at me. Look into my eyes. It is I. Do not be afraid. I told you that I would rise."

You are there with the risen Jesus. It is just the two of you. You are right next to him. Jesus looks deep into your eyes with great love. He asks you once again, "Who do you say that I am?"

Answer the question from your heart. Then, have the courage to ask, "Who do you say that *I* am, Lord?" Let him respond. Ask him to reveal how he sees you.

After a little while he looks at you and asks, "Do you love me?" Answer from your heart. Answer the question in whatever way is natural.

Then, have the courage to ask him the same question: "Do you love me?" Let him respond. Ask him to reveal how he feels for you.

Then, imagine that you feel *him*. You feel *his* hand. With his right hand he squeezes your left hand. You see those eyes, the eyes you have looked into throughout this Lent. You are overcome with love and trust.

Looking deep into your eyes, Jesus says to you: "Look at me. Trust me. Do not be afraid. I will be with you ... *forever*. I am here. I am with you. All I ask is this: Do not take your eyes off me."

He is risen. He is with you. He never leaves.

Return to the campfire from time to time in your prayer.

Review your journal from this Lent.

You have come to *personally know* the God of

the universe, who *promises* to be with you *always*.

Lean on him ... remember him ...

receive his blessing every day:

"Look at me. Trust me. Do not be afraid.

I will be with you ... *forever*. I am here.

I am with you. All I ask is this:

Don't take your eyes off me."

"They went toward the tomb. They both ran."

—JOHN 20:3-4

Notes

1   Joseph Whelan, "Fall in Love," *IgnatianSpirituality.com* (blog), *Loyola Press.*

2   Benedict XVI, *Deus Caritas Est* (December 25, 2005), 1.

3   The RSV-2CE uses the term "wilderness" in Luke 4:2.

4   Benedict XVI, 18.

5   Ibid., 2.

6   Ibid., 18.

7   Whelan, "Fall in Love."

8   Timother M. Gallagher, *Meditation and Contemplation: An Ignatian Guide to Praying with Scripture* (New York: Crossroad, 2008), Kindle.

9   Benedict XVI, 2.

10   Whelan, "Fall in Love."

11   Ibid.

12   Benedict XVI, 1.

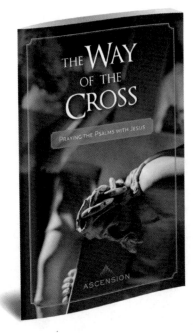

The Way of the Cross:
Praying the Psalms with Jesus

Experience the Way of the Cross as you never have before. Rather than meditating *about* Christ's journey to the Cross, pray *with* him.

Jesus, as an observant Jewish man, would have prayed the Psalms throughout the day and drawn strength and peace from them.

In *The Way of the Cross: Praying the Psalms with Jesus,* Fr. Mark Toups invites us to step closer to Christ and pray beside him, drawing strength from Scripture during his last moments before the Crucifixion.

Each station features a short reading from Scripture, a brief meditation, and a psalm to pray with Christ.

THE ASCENSION
Lenten
Companion

Fine Art Print Collection

Bringing the sacred art from the *Lenten Companion*
into your home is the perfect way to welcome Jesus into
your heart, not only during Lent but all year long.

Choose from nine original oil paintings from Mike Moyers,
created exclusively for

The Ascension Lenten Companion

Visit AscensionPress.com to learn more.